James J. Hennessy, PhD
Nathaniel J. Pallone, PhD
Editors

Drug Courts in Operation: Current Research

Drug Courts in Operation: Current Research has been co-published simultaneously as *Journal of Offender Rehabilitation*, Volume 33, Number 4 2001.

Pre-publication
REVIEWS,
COMMENTARIES,
EVALUATIONS

" As one of the founders of the drug court movement, I can testify that Dr. Hennessy's book represents the highest level of sophistication in this field. Cutting-edge studies involving race, gender, and family issues are reviewed in this comprehensive textbook. I was especially impressed by Dr. Adela Beckerman's chapter on race and gender issues. Rather than merely stressing the patient's need for compliance, she shows how a drug court program can be a vehicle to develop specific programs for women and African Americans."

Michael O. Smith, MD
Director, Lincoln Recovery Center
Bronx, New York
Assistant Clinical Professor
of Psychiatry

More pre-publication
REVIEWS, COMMENTARIES, EVALUATIONS . . .

"AN OUTSTANDING COMPOSITE OF EVALUATIONS AND THEIR IMPACT ON THE DRUG COURT FIELD. As the number of drug courts multiply across the nation, attention will continue to focus on the success of these innovative programs and what makes them successful. The research that Dr. Hennessy has compiled is impressive and the results, compelling."

C. West Huddleston, III, Director,
The National Drug Court Institute, Alexandria, Virginia

The Haworth Press, Inc.

Drug Courts in Operation: Current Research

Drug Courts in Operation: Current Research has been co-published simultaneously as *Journal of Offender Rehabilitation*, Volume 33, Number 4 2001.

The *Journal of Offender Rehabilitation* Monographic "Separates"

Below is a list of "separates," which in serials librarianship means a special issue simultaneously published as a special journal issue or double-issue *and* as a "separate" hardbound monograph. (This is a format which we also call a "DocuSerial.")

"Separates" are published because specialized libraries or professionals may wish to purchase a specific thematic issue by itself in a format which can be separately cataloged and shelved, as opposed to purchasing the journal on an on-going basis. Faculty members may also more easily consider a "separate" for classroom adoption.

"Separates" are carefully classified separately with the major book jobbers so that the journal tie-in can be noted on new book order slips to avoid duplicate purchasing.

You may wish to visit Haworth's website at . . .

http://www.HaworthPress.com

. . . to search our online catalog for complete tables of contents of these separates and related publications.

You may also call 1-800-HAWORTH (outside US/Canada: 607-722-5857), or Fax 1-800-895-0582 (outside US/Canada: 607-771-0012), or e-mail at:

getinfo@haworthpressinc.com

Drug Courts in Operation: Current Research, edited by James J. Hennessy, PhD, and Nathaniel J. Pallone, PhD (Vol. 33, No. 4, 2001). *"As one of the founders of the drug court movement, I can testify that Dr. Hennessy's book represents the highest level of sophistication in this field."* (Michael O. Smith, MD, Director, Lincoln Recovery Center, Bronx, New York: Assistant Clinical Professor of Psychiatry, Cornell University Medical School)

Family Empowerment as an Intervention Strategy in Juvenile Delinquency, edited by Richard Dembo, PhD, and Nathaniel J. Pallone, PhD (Vol. 33, No. 1, 2001). *"A hands-on book. . . . Provides detailed guidelines for counselors regarding implementation of the FEI curriculum . . . accurately describes the scope of counselor responsibilities and the nature of treatment interventions. Unique in its coverage of counselor competencies and training/supervision needs. Innovative and based on solid empirical evidence."* (Roger H. Peters, PhD, Professor, University of South Florida, Tampa)

Race, Ethnicity, Sexual Orientation, Violent Crime: The Realities and the Myths, edited by Nathaniel J. Pallone, PhD (Vol. 30, No. 1/2, 1999). *"A fascinating book which illuminates the complexity of race as it applies to the criminal justice system and the myths and political correctness that have shrouded the real truth. . . . I highly recommend this book for those who study causes of crime in minority populations."* (Joseph R. Carlson, PhD, Associate Professor, University of Nebraska at Kearney)

Sex Offender Treatment: Biological Dysfunction, Intrapsychic Conflict, Interpersonal Violence, edited by Eli Coleman, PhD, S. Margretta Dwyer, MA, and Nathaniel J. Pallone, PhD (Vol. 23, No. 3/4, 1996). *"Offers a review of current assessment and treatment theory while addressing critical issues such as standards of care, use of phallometry, and working with specialized populations such as exhibitionists and developmentally disabled clients. . . . A valuable addition to the reader's professional library."* (Robert E. Freeman-Longo, MRC, LPC, Director, The Safer Society Press)

The Psychobiology of Aggression: Engines, Measurement, Control, edited by Marc Hillbrand, PhD, and Nathaniel J. Pallone, PhD (Vol. 21, No. 3/4, 1995). *"A comprehensive sourcebook for the increasing dialogue between psychobiologists, neuropsychiatrists, and those interested in a full understanding of the dynamics and control of criminal aggression."* (Criminal Justice Review)

Young Victims, Young Offenders: Current Issues in Policy and Treatment, edited by Nathaniel J. Pallone, PhD (Vol. 21, No. 1/2, 1994). *"Extremely practical. . . . Aims to increase knowledge about the patterns of youthful offenders and give help in designing programs of prevention and* rehabilitation." (S. Margretta Dwyer, Director of Sex Offender Treatment Program, Department of Family Practice, University of Minnesota)

Sex Offender Treatment: Psychological and Medical Approaches, edited by Eli Coleman, PhD, S. Margretta Dwyer, and Nathaniel J. Pallone, PhD (Vol. 18, No. 3/4, 1992). *"Summarizes research worldwide on the various approaches to treating sex offenders for both researchers and clinicians." (SciTech Book News)*

The Clinical Treatment of the Criminal Offender in Outpatient Mental Health Settings: New and Emerging Perspectives, edited by Sol Chaneles, PhD, and Nathaniel J. Pallone, PhD (Vol. 15, No. 1, 1990). *"The clinical professional concerned with the outpatient treatment of the criminal offender will find this book informative and useful." (Criminal Justice Review)*

Older Offenders: Current Trends, edited by Sol Chaneles, PhD, and Cathleen Burnett, PhD (Vol. 13, No. 2, 1985). *"Broad in scope and should provide a fruitful beginning for future discussion and exploration." (Criminal Justice Review)*

Prisons and Prisoners: Historical Documents, edited by Sol Chaneles, PhD (Vol. 10, No. 1/2, 1985). *"May help all of us . . . to gain some understanding as to why prisons have resisted change for over 300 years. . . . Very challenging and very disturbing." (Public Offender Counseling Association)*

Gender Issues, Sex Offenses, and Criminal Justice: Current Trends, edited by Sol Chaneles, PhD (Vol. 9, No. 1/2, 1984). *"The contributions of the work will be readily apparent to any reader interested in an interdisciplinary approach to criminology and women's studies." (Criminal Justice Review)*

Current Trends in Correctional Education: Theory and Practice, edited by Sol Chaneles, PhD (Vol. 7, No. 3/4, 1983). *"A laudable presentation of educational issues in relation to corrections." (International Journal of Offender Therapy and Comparative Criminology)*

Counseling Juvenile Offenders in Institutional Settings, edited by Sol Chaneles, PhD (Vol. 6, No. 3, 1983). *"Covers a variety of settings and approaches, from juvenile awareness programs, day care, and vocational rehabilitation to actual incarceration in juvenile and adult institutions. . . . Good coverage of the subject." (Canada's Mental Health)*

Strategies of Intervention with Public Offenders, edited by Sol Chaneles, PhD (Vol. 6, No. 1/2, 1982). *"The information presented is well-organized and should prove useful to the practitioner, the student, or for use in in-service training." (The Police Chief)*

∞ ALL HAWORTH BOOKS AND JOURNALS
ARE PRINTED ON CERTIFIED
ACID-FREE PAPER

Drug Courts in Operation: Current Research

James J. Hennessy
Nathaniel J. Pallone
Editors

Drug Courts in Operation: Current Research has been co-published simultaneously as *Journal of Offender Rehabilitation*, Volume 33, Number 4 2001.

The Haworth Press, Inc.
New York • London • Oxford

Drug Courts in Operation: Current Research has been co-published simultaneously as *Journal of Offender Rehabilitation*™, Volume 33, Number 4 2001.

© 2001 by The Haworth Press, Inc. All rights reserved. No part of this work may be reproduced or utilized in any form or by any means, electronic or mechanical, including photocopying, microfilm and recording, or by any information storage and retrieval system, without permission in writing from the publisher. Printed in the United States of America.

The development, preparation, and publication of this work has been undertaken with great care. However, the publisher, employees, editors, and agents of The Haworth Press and all imprints of The Haworth Press, Inc., including The Haworth Medical Press® and Pharmaceutical Products Press®, are not responsible for any errors contained herein or for consequences that may ensue from use of materials or information contained in this work. Opinions expressed by the author(s) are not necessarily those of The Haworth Press, Inc.

Cover design by Thomas J. Mayshock Jr.

Library of Congress Cataloging-in-Publication Data

Drug courts in operation : current research / James J. Hennessy, Nathaniel J. Pallone, editors.
    p. cm.
"Co-published simultaneously as Journal of offender rehabilitation, volume 33, number 4, 2001."
Includes bibliographical references and index.
    ISBN 0-7890-1694-X (hard : alk. paper) – ISBN 0-7890-1695-8 (pbk. : alk. paper)
    1. Drug courts–United States. 2. Drug abuse–Treatment–Law and legislation–United States. 3. Narcotic addicts–Rehabilitation–United States. I. Hennessy, James, 1942- II. Pallone, Nathaniel J. III. Journal of offender rehabilitation.

KF3890 .D776 2002
345.73'0277–dc21

2002017209

Indexing, Abstracting & Website/Internet Coverage

This section provides you with a list of major indexing & abstracting services. That is to say, each service began covering this periodical during the year noted in the right column. Most Websites which are listed below have indicated that they will either post, disseminate, compile, archive, cite or alert their own Website users with research-based content from this work. (This list is as current as the copyright date of this publication.)

Abstracting, Website/Indexing Coverage . . . . Year When Coverage Began

- *BUBL Information Service, an Internet-based Information Service for the UK higher education community* <http://bubl.ac.uk/> 1995

- *CNPIEC Reference Guide: Chinese National Directory of Foreign Periodicals* 1996

- *Criminal Justice Abstracts* 1986

- *Criminal Justice Periodical Index* 1982

- *e-psyche, LLC <www.e-psyche.net>* 1999

- *ERIC Clearinghouse on Counseling and Student Services (ERIC/CASS)* 1983

- *Expanded Academic ASAP <www.galegroup.com>* 1999

- *Family and Society Studies Worldwide <www.nisc.com>* 1996

- *Family Violence & Sexual Assault Bulletin* 1992

(continued)

- *FINDEX <www.publist.com>* 1999
- *Gay & Lesbian Abstracts <www.nisc.com>* 2001
- *IBZ International Bibliography of Periodical Literature <www.saur.de>* 1996
- *Index Guide to College Journals (core list compiled by integrating 48 indexes frequently used to support undergraduate programs in small to medium sized libraries)* 1999
- *Index to Periodical Articles Related to Law* 1991
- *National Clearinghouse on Child Abuse & Neglect Information Documents Database <www.calib.com/nccanch>* 2001
- *National Criminal Justice Reference Service <www.ncjrs.org>* 1982
- *NIAAA Alcohol and Alcohol Problems Science Database (ETOH) <http://etoh.niaaa.nih.gov>* 1995
- *Psychological Abstracts (PsycINFO) <www.apa.org>* 1999
- *Referativnyi Zhurnal (Abstracts Journal of the All-Russian Institute of Scientific and Technical Information–in Russian)* ... 1986
- *Sage Urban Studies Abstracts (SUSA)* 1992
- *Social Sciences Index (from Volume 1 and continuing) <www.hwwilson.com>* 1999
- *Social Services Abstracts <www.csa.com>* 1982
- *Social Work Abstracts <www.silverplatter.com/catalog/swab.htm>* 1982
- *Sociological Abstracts (SA) <www.csa.com>* 1982
- *Special Educational Needs Abstracts* 1989
- *Studies on Women Abstracts* 1998
- *Violence and Abuse Abstracts: A Review of Current Literature on Interpersonal Violence (VAA)* 1994

Special Bibliographic Notes related to special journal issues (separates) and indexing/abstracting:

- indexing/abstracting services in this list will also cover material in any "separate" that is co-published simultaneously with Haworth's special thematic journal issue or DocuSerial. Indexing/abstracting usually covers material at the article/chapter level.
- monographic co-editions are intended for either non-subscribers or libraries which intend to purchase a second copy for their circulating collections.
- monographic co-editions are reported to all jobbers/wholesalers/approval plans. The source journal is listed as the "series" to assist the prevention of duplicate purchasing in the same manner utilized for books-in-series.
- to facilitate user/access services all indexing/abstracting services are encouraged to utilize the co-indexing entry note indicated at the bottom of the first page of each article/chapter/contribution.
- this is intended to assist a library user of any reference tool (whether print, electronic, online, or CD-ROM) to locate the monographic version if the library has purchased this version but not a subscription to the source journal.
- individual articles/chapters in any Haworth publication are also available through the Haworth Document Delivery Service (HDDS).

Drug Courts in Operation: Current Research

CONTENTS

Introduction: Drug Courts in Operation   1
    JAMES J. HENNESSY
    Fordham University

The "Drug Court Strengthening Families" Program   11
    TK LOGAN
    Center on Drug and Alcohol Research, University of Kentucky
    CARL LEUKEFELD
    Center on Drug and Alcohol Research, University of Kentucky
    LISA MINTON
    Kentucky Administrative Office of the Courts
    JOANIE ABRAHMSON
    Kentucky Administrative Office of the Courts
    REBECCA HUGHES
    Center on Drug and Alcohol Research, University of Kentucky

Issues of Race and Gender in Court-Ordered Substance Abuse Treatment   45
    ADELA BECKERMAN
    Nova Southeastern University
    LEONARD FONTANA
    Broward Community College

Treatment "Dosage" Effects in Drug Court Programs   63
    ROGER H. PETERS
    University of South Florida
    AMIE L. HAAS
    University of South Florida
    W. MICHAEL HUNT
    University of South Florida

Employment Issues Among Court Participants   73

   MICHELE STATON

   University of Kentucky Center on Drug and Alcohol Research

   ALLISON MATEYOKE

   University of Kentucky Center on Drug and Alcohol Research

   CARL LEUKEFELD

   University of Kentucky Center on Drug and Alcohol Research

   JENNIFER COLE

   University of Kentucky Center on Drug and Alcohol Research

   HOLLY HOPPER

   University of Kentucky Center on Drug and Alcohol Research

   TK LOGAN

   University of Kentucky Center on Drug and Alcohol Research

   LISA MINTON

   Kentucky Administrative Office of the Courts

Predictors of Engagement in Court-Mandated Treatment: Findings at the Brooklyn Treatment Court, 1996-2000   87

   MICHAEL REMPEL

   Center for Court Innovation

   CHRISTINE DEPIES DESTEFANO

   Urban Institute, Justice Policy Center

Index   125

ABOUT THE EDITORS

James J. Hennessy, PhD, is Professor and former Chairperson for the Division of Psychological and Educational Services, Graduate School of Education, Fordham University. His publications include *Criminal Behavior: A Process Psychology Analysis, Fraud and Fallible Judgment: Varieties of Deception in the Social and Behavioral Sciences*, and *Tinder-Box Criminal Aggression: Neuropsychology, Demography, Phenomenology*. He also serves as an independent evaluation consultant to drug courts in the cities of Yonkers and Mount Vernon in Westchester County, New York.

Nathaniel J. Pallone, PhD, editor-in-chief of the *Journal of Offender Rehabilitation*, is University Distinguished Professor (Psychology), Center of Alcohol Studies, at Rutgers–The State University of New Jersey, where he previously served as dean and as academic vice president.

Introduction:
Drug Courts in Operation

JAMES J. HENNESSY

Fordham University

ABSTRACT This introduction to the volume on drug treatment courts reviews, in brief, the history of the nation's recent "war on drugs," underscoring oscillations between punitive and rehabilitation emphases with particular focus on the history of drug courts as a principal treatment alternative that integrates both rehabilitation and punitive aspects. Data on the extent both of drug use and abuse and of arrests for illicit use and abuse are reviewed, and the contents of the volume are adumbrated. *[Article copies available for a fee from The Haworth Document Delivery Service: 1-800-HAWORTH. E-mail address: <getinfo@haworthpressinc.com> Website: <http://www.HaworthPress.com> © 2001 by The Haworth Press, Inc. All rights reserved.]*

KEYWORDS Alternatives to incarceration, drug court history, coercive treatment, incarceration rates, therapeutic jurisprudence

Drug use and abuse continue to be vexing problems in America. Attitudes and policies that view drug use as a disorder (and eventually a disease) that is best dealt with by "treatment" vie with beliefs and policies that view drug use as a crime warranting severe sanctions, up to and including imprisonment for long periods. These conflicting views have held sway at different times in the

United States, with the "treatment" side holding an edge through the 1960s and the "get tough" side prevailing from the early 1970s through the 1990s. Once again, the pendulum seems to be swinging, but this time to a position that recognizes that while for many people drug use is an addiction in need of treatment, it is also a crime for which reasonable sanctions are appropriately administered through the criminal justice system. This change in perspective is exemplified in two seemingly related but substantively different movements emerging today, namely decriminalization and drug treatment courts. Before considering these two, a brief review of the social and political factors that are empowering them is provided.

THE WAR ON DRUGS

After three decades of a "war on drugs" in the United States, a time during which drug use became almost the norm among large segments of the population, and during which time the prison population increased more than three fold, a change in thinking about the "drug problem" in America is slowly coming about. The change is a function of many factors, none of which by itself is likely the most important. In the 1970s, sparked in part by the social unrest on college campuses that manifest itself in the open use of marijuana, LSD, and other psychedelic stimulants, in part by the high rates of addictions among military personnel returning from the war in Southeast Asia, and in part by the growing availability of illegal drugs of all kinds in the inner cities, the federal government began its "war on drugs" by attacking directly drug manufacture in Asia and South America, and by urging states to increase the penalties for drug-related crimes at home. States were encouraged to criminalize, prosecute, and punish drug possession and drug use, as well as drug sale. The impact of the "get tough" policies on the criminal justice system has been stunning, as can be readily observed in the exponential growth in the number of persons under supervision in the United States at the turn of the millennium. In 1970, the incarceration rate in the United States was 96 per 100,000 residents; in 1999, the rate had climbed to 452 per 100,000, with incarcerations for violent crimes (often "lubricated" by drug use by both the offender and perpetrator) and drug offenses making the greatest contribution to the increase. Indeed, in the federal prison system, the increase in the percent of inmates serving time for drug offenses rose from 16.3% in 1970 (when the population under sentence was 20,686) to 58.9% in 1998 (when the population under sentence rose to 95,522) (Maguire & Pastore, 1999, p. 505).

Recent Bureau of Justice Statistics findings (Beck & Karberg, 2001) indicate that at year end 1999, 6.3 million people were in the correctional population in the United States, with approximately 1.3 million in physical custody in civilian state and federal prisons, and almost 700,000 in jails. Of the approximately 2 million people incarcerated in civilian facilities in 1999, over 10% were imprisoned on drug offenses only (N = 236,8000); however, 83% of all prisoners surveyed in 1997 indicated that they had used illegal drugs in their pasts, with approximately 70% admitting to regular use in the month preceding arrest, and 33% indicating drug use at the time of the offense for which they were arrested. Over 50% of prisoners incarcerated for murder and assault indicated that they had been under the influence of drugs at the time of the offense, with approximately 35% of those imprisoned for drug offenses so indicating (Maguire & Pastore, 1999, 509). Were appropriate assessments conducted, it is likely that a high proportion of "regular" users would be found to be substance abusers or addicts who upon release would return to their former ways, especially given that fewer than one-third of drug-involved inmates participate in a formal treatment program while incarcerated.

The failure of the "war on drugs" can be encountered outside the walls of prisons as well. Drug offenses now constitute over 10% of offenses leading to arrest in the United States, up from 5% in 1980. Of the 1.58 million drug arrests in 1998, 80% were for drug possession (as different from drug sale and manufacture), a rate similar to 1981 when only 559,300 such arrests were made. A recent report released by the National Research Council, the research arm of the National Academy of Sciences, was critical of the efforts to curb the illegal "drug market" and of the attempts to offer as prevention strategies programs for which there was no evidence of validity. According to a Reuters news release (3/29/01), the report concluded that because reliable data on illegal drug consumption and the cost of illicit drugs were unavailable, there was no way of knowing whether the $12 billion annually spent on drug enforcement was yielding any detectable effects. The report pointed to large holes in the information available to inform the nation's health policy. Popular prevention programs such as D.A.R.E. are under intense criticism both from the NRC and from local schools that have incorporated these programs into their curriculum because of the almost complete absence of evidence supporting the effectiveness of these programs.

The Center for Substance Abuse Prevention (CSAP), a division of the Substance Abuse and Mental Health Services Administration (SAMHSA), is the leading federal agency in the drug prevention effort, yet it funds only a small number of demonstration and replication programs annually. In fiscal year 2001, CSAP allocated $175 million to prevention, out of a $2.1 billion SAMHSA budget. The bulk of SAMHSA funding ($1.7 billion) is designated as block grants to states. As with the question raised by the NRC regarding the investment in drug enforcement, questions may be raised regarding the impact of efforts toward treatment and prevention.

According to the recently released SAMHSA 1999 National Household Drug Abuse Survey (SAMHSA, 2001), an estimated 14.8 million Americans were illicit drug users in 1999 (respondents to a survey who indicated that they had used an illicit drug during the month prior to interview), representing 6.7 percent of the population 12 years old and older. Marijuana was the most commonly used illicit drug, used by 75 percent of drug users. The majority specified marijuana as the only drug used; however, 43 percent (an estimated 6.4 million Americans) used illicit drugs other than marijuana and hashish, with or without the use of marijuana, including four million who were using psychotherapeutics non-medically (representing 1.8 percent of the population age 12 and older). An estimated 1.5 million were current cocaine users, approximately 900,000 were current hallucinogen users, and an estimated 200,000 were heroin users. When illicit drug use was inflected by age, SAMHSA reported that 10.9 percent of youth aged 12-17 had used an illicit drug within the 30 days prior to interview, including 7.7 percent who had used marijuana, and 5.3 percent who had used illicit drugs other than marijuana. The cohort of 18-20-year-olds had the highest rate of illicit drug use (between 20 and 21 percent), with use dominated by marijuana. When inflected by race, drug use was found to differ only slightly among the major racial/ethnic groups, with 6.6 percent for whites, 6.8 percent for Hispanics, and 7.7 percent for blacks. Persons reporting being multiracial had the highest rate at 11.2 percent. As to the success of prevention and enforcement efforts directed toward secondary students, 56.5 percent of youths age 12-17 reported marijuana was easy to obtain, and 15.6 percent of youths reported being approached by someone selling drugs during the 30 days prior to the interview.

A "positive" finding in the survey was that the percent of the population age 12 and older using illicit drugs in the month prior to interview did not change significantly between 1998 and 1999 (6.2 percent in 1998 and 7.0 percent in 1999). But that positive note came after findings that indicate that between 1990 and 1999, the number of first-time users of marijuana increased 63% (from 1,437,000 in 1990 to 2,338,000), the number of cocaine users by 37%, users of inhalants by 154%, and of stimulants by 165%. Those increases contrast with the 44% increase in first-time tobacco users 1990 to 1999. While there may now be a leveling off in the growth of the percent of new users, the data certainly suggest that illicit drug use continued to grow at substantial rates during the years in which billions of dollars were being spent on drug enforcement and the incarceration of tens of thousands of drug offenders, most of whom were low-level users. Two alternatives to the "get tough" position have emerged over the past decade, emerging first in south Florida, followed by

California, and now by most states. Those alternatives incorporate "treatment" as an integral component of the penal and rehabilitative emphases of the criminal justice system.

TREATMENT ALTERNATIVES TO INCARCERATION

The two current models for responding to the drug problem in America both strive to reduce the need to incarcerate drug users who have been arrested for drug use, possession, and other drug-related misdemeanor offenses. The first model, which is the focus of this special issue, is the drug treatment court. While an operational model only since 1989, drug treatment courts are considered to be the most innovative, comprehensive, and successful alternatives to incarceration yet developed. The "drug courts" grew from a grassroots, in-the-courthouse realization that the turnstile in the criminal justice system of repeated incarcerations following repeated arrests of habituated drug users was clogging the system and costing millions of dollars in ineffective efforts to rehabilitate addicted chronic offenders. The Miami-Dade County Circuit Court was the first court to integrate a mandatory "treatment" component into the supervisory responsibilities of the court. The court relied upon the authority of the judge to develop and supervise a comprehensive, community-based rehabilitation and supervision program intended to use the "coercive powers" of the court to compel "participants" (a.k.a., offenders) to abide by the treatment plan in order to avoid incarceration. The essence of drug courts today continues to be the coercive power of the court to impose sanctions, including incarceration, on participants who deviate from the treatment plan.

Drug treatment courts, according to Hore, Schma, and Rosenthal (1999) emerged from wide recognition that traditional criminal justice methods of incarceration, probation, or supervised parole have not had great impact on drug use or on drug-related crime. These authors suggested that drug court unknowingly applied the concept of "therapeutic jurisprudence" in the formulation of early courts. Therapeutic jurisprudence has been defined variously as (a) the study of the extent to which substantive rules, legal procedures, and the roles of lawyers and judges produce therapeutic or antitherapeutic consequences for individuals involved in the legal process; (b) the use of social science to study the extent to which a legal rule or practice promotes the psychological and physical well-being of the people it affects, and (c) the study of the role of law as a therapeutic agent (Hore, Schma, & Rosenthal 1999, pp. 442-444). Therapeutic jurisprudence and its actualization in drug courts recognize that drug use is not solely a criminal justice/law enforcement problem but also a public health problem with deep roots in the community.

As of early 2001, more than 1,000 drug treatment courts were in operation or in the planning stage in all 50 states, most U.S. territories, many Native American Tribal Courts, and in the federal court system (Huddleston, 2001). Although each jurisdiction tailors its specific drug court policies and procedures to accommodate local conditions and needs, all share a commitment to several "key components" and to the proactive need to obtain empirical data to assess the impact of these courts.

Of the critical components, the first is that drug courts integrate alcohol and other drug treatment services with criminal justice system case processing by including a broad-based planning group that develops policies, processes, and procedures using a shared-decision-making model. Drug courts provide a non-adversarial approach (another key component) in which prosecutors and defense counsel collaborate on program design and operation and in which they limit their traditional "advocacy" roles to staffing sessions and other non-court settings. Policies and procedures for identifying "eligible" participants assure early identification and assessment of participants, which allows for almost-immediate enrollment in a treatment program. (In those jurisdictions receiving federal funding to plan, implement, or enhance drug court, offenders having any conviction for violent crimes are not eligible to participate.) The court has available to it a full spectrum of services, ranging from detoxification programs to long-term, inpatient care; treatment services are expected to be comprehensive, and to have quality-control and accountability systems in place. Regular reporting back to the drug court team is part of the contract between treatment providers and the court. By treating addiction as a biopsychosocial issue, drug courts and their partners ask those who work in the criminal justice system to alter their orientation away from the traditional role of the court; and to view the process as therapeutic and treatment-oriented instead of punitive in nature (Hore, Schma, Rosenthal, 1999).

From a participant's perspective, drug court involvement requires regular court appearances (generally weekly in the early phases of involvement), frequent and random drug testing at treatment sites and in court, and full compliance with the treatment regime, which often includes attendance at AA/NA-like meetings. As the participant moves into the middle and later phases of drug court program, vocational and educational services may be introduced if there is need for them. "Graduation" from drug court (usually after 12 or more months) requires that the participant remained "clean and sober" for 12 consecutive months, earned a high school diploma or GED, and obtained a job. Should a participant fail a drug test, fail to attend treatment sessions, or in other ways not follow the mandated program, a series of sanctions is available to the court. Sanctions may include a monetary fine, a certain number of hours of community service, a requirement for more frequent court and/or treatment sessions, and incarceration for a specified period of time. If a participant is deemed to be failing in the drug court (a decision arrived at by the team), the participant may be dropped from the program and remanded back to the court of original jurisdiction for a hearing, trial, or sentencing on an already-pled-to conviction. It is this on going coercive power that renders the drug court distinct from other diversion programs, including that being implemented in California following passage of Proposition 36 last November.

The drug court concept was implemented to its greatest extent in California, where courts were established in many counties across the breadth and length of the state. Los Angeles and San Diego operate drug courts that are among the largest in the country. In 1999, prompted by advocates of the decriminalization of drug use, a ballot initiative was proposed that eventually was voted on in 2000, and passed by a large majority vote. The initiative, Proposition 36, was promoted as a more realistic, cost-effective model for dealing with drug offenders. Unlike the drug court model which requires that a participant be a habituated user with no prior felony convictions, Proposition 36 applies to all first- and second-time drug possession offenders, except for those convicted of a non-drug crime concurrent with the drug possession charge, or those having a prior conviction for a violent felony unless the person has been out of prison and committed no felonies for five years. All eligible offenders are diverted to mandated treatment and placed on probation. However, incarceration is not an option for the court; as opponents of the proposition had argued, the proposition effectively decriminalized possession of most illegal drugs, including heroin, crack cocaine, and methamphetamines. It is much too soon to assess the impact of Proposition 36, other than to suggest that it will likely lessen the number of cases referred to the drug court system in California, and will likely lead to similar proposals in other states.

The future of drug courts was made less certain nationally with the change in administrations and with the appointment of an opponent of the "treatment" view as attorney general. As this issue was going to press, news reports circulated indicating that the Drug Court Program Office, Department of Justice, would continue to funded, assuring that planning activities would be supported through 2002. If decisions about that future are based on empirical evidence, then the future of drug courts may be assured.

One key component of drug courts established early on was that drug courts monitor and evaluate their activities. Evaluation is built into a drug court during the planning phase, and systematic data collection and process assessment are initiated at the onset of the court and continue from thereon. That component has allowed for the generation of numerous published studies of the impact and effects of drug courts, including the articles included in this volume. The findings generally are strongly supportive of claims of effectiveness in a variety of domains. Summaries of the impact literature were provided by Belenko (1998, 1999) and by the Drug Court Clearinghouse and Technical assistance Project at American University (1998). The evidence provided indicates that drug court participants remain "clean and sober," have lower recidivism rates, and lower rearrest rates. "The original goals for drug courts . . . are being achieved, with recidivism rates substantially reduced for graduates . . . drug usage rates for defendants while they are participating in the drug court are . . . dramatically below the rate observed for non-drug court offenders. The 'outcomes' that drug courts are achieving go far beyond these original goals, however: the birth of more than 500 drug-free babies to drug court participants; the unification of hundreds of families . . ." (American University, 1998, p. 1). Findings about impact and effectiveness have been published primarily in journals and monographs published in and for the drug court community. With this volume, we hope to inform the broader offender rehabilitation community about the research being conducted in drug courts around the country. The five articles reported herein represent the variety of study designs and foci that are being used to assess need for drug courts (TK Logan and associates), treatment issues that may affect outcomes (Beckerman & Fontana and Peters, Haas, & Hunt), real-world employment issues that affect participation (Staton and associates), and, finally, factors that predict treatment engagement (Rempel & DeStefano).

In the first article, TK Logan and her colleagues at the Center on Drug and Alcohol Research at the University of Kentucky examine the risk factors children are exposed to while living with drug-using parents and then introduce a program designed to strengthen families so as to reduce the impact of those factors. The article incorporates several methodologies, including needs assessment, process evaluation employing qualitative methods, and more traditional outcome evaluation employing a control-group design. The findings argue for the importance of including at-risk children of drug court participants in the treatment process.

In the next article, Beckerman and Fontana focus on a difficult confound in the treatment process, namely the impact of race and gender on treatment. Their analysis of the need for cultural- and gender-specific treatments was reinforced by their findings of significant differences in time in treatment and incidence of clean drug test results. They challenge the claim that failure to graduate results from willful defiance of judicial authority, and suggest instead that flaws in the design of treatment programs be addressed. The article by Peters, Haas, and Hunt examines the links between time in treatment (a measure of treatment dosage) and arrest rates at 12 and 30 months post-treatment. Their finding of a "striking linear relationship" between treatment dosage and rearrest rates led to recommendations for further research to assess the relations between dosage and other drug court outcomes, such as employment and health care utilization.

Staton and her colleagues at the Center on Drug and Alcohol Research, University of Kentucky, used a focus group design to explore issues that affect how drug court participants balance (or have difficulty balancing) job responsibilities with the requirements of regular court appearances and treatment sessions. Participants often begin to view their job as their priority, sacrificing treatment and court appearances in order to preserve their jobs. But as I witnessed recently, the court views faithful adherence to its mandates as the priority that keeps the participant out of jail, thus allowing the participant the opportunity to work. Staton et al. offer recommendations that may ease this conflict.

In the final article, Rempel and DeStefano report on their sophisticated multivariate analyses of factors that "predict" engagement in treatment as measured by completion of the first phase of a three-phase program at the Brooklyn (NY) Treatment Court. That court is the largest drug court in the country, handling drug-addicted defendants arrested on felony drug charges. Their findings regarding the power of legal coercion should be considered by those jurisdictions contemplating following California's move to decouple treatment from intrusive sanctions.

As the articles in this volume amply demonstrate, the effects of drug treatment courts come about from a complex interaction among treatment providers, the defense bar, prosecutors, the court, and the defendant-client. The unique, non-adversarial attitude of "we are all here to help you" enacted by those working in drug courts defines this kind of court as being different from other courts. I have had the good fortune of observing and participating in this collegial arena in two drug courts on whose planning and implementation teams I serve. I am deeply indebted to the Honorable Brenda Dowery-Rodriquez, Chief Judge, City Court of Mount Vernon, and her team led by Shawyn Patterson-Howard, and to the Honorable Arthur J. ("Mike") Doran, Chief Judge, City Court of Yonkers, and his team led by Sharon Davis for the opportunity these Courts have given me to participate in the establishment of drug courts in their communities. With full recognition that anecdotes cannot substitute for rigorous, empirical analysis, I became acutely aware of the importance of teamwork, team spirit, and the need to change long-held beliefs and attitudes in the building of effective drug courts. My experiences, and the findings reported in the articles in this volume, indicate that the power and effectiveness of drug courts arise not from a placebo or novelty effect but from the careful planning and training that are essential elements in the drug court movement.

A concern that will arise as states such as New York begin to establish drug treatment courts in virtually every jurisdiction in the state is that the special character that comes from being a part of something that is different may be vitiated as these courts become institutionalized and regimented. The pioneer spirit of the early drug court movement must eventually yield to an acceptance of greater oversight and regulation. One can only hope that in that transformation, the special essence of the program will not be destroyed. Routinization or institutionalization of drug treatment courts should be accompanied by a strong commitment to the 10 key components that thus far have so successfully guided the many courts operating today.

REFERENCES

Belenko, S. (1998). Research on drug courts: a critical review. *National Drug Court Institute Review*, *1*(1), 1-42.
Belenko, S. (1999). Research on drug courts: a critical review 1999 update. *National Drug Court Institute Review*, 2 (2), 1-58.
Drug Court Clearinghouse and Technical Assistance Project. (1998). *Looking at a decade of drug courts*. U.S. Department of Justice, Drug Court Program Office. Washington, DC: USGPO.
Hore, P. F., Schma, W. G., & Rosenthal, J. T. (1999). Therapeutic jurisprudence and the drug treatment court movement: revolutionizing the criminal justice system's response to drug abuse and crime in America. *Notre Dame Law Review*, 74, 439-537.
Huddleston, C. W. (2001, April). Drug courts: Philosophy and history. Paper presented at the *National Drug Court Institute Adult Drug Court Skills Based Planning Workshop*, Jacksonville, FL.
Maguire, K., & Pastore, A. (1999). *Sourcebook of Criminal Justice Statistics–1998*. US. Department of Justice, Bureau of Justice Statistics. Washington, DC: USGPO.
Substance Abuse and Mental Health Services Administration. (2001). The 1999 National Household Survey on Drug Abuse. U.S. Department of Health and Human Services, Substance Abuse and Mental Health Services Administration. Washington, DC: Author.

AUTHOR'S NOTES

James J. Hennessy, PhD, is a professor and former chair, Division of Psychological and Educational Services, Graduate School of Education, Fordham University. His books include *Criminal Behavior: A Process Psychology Analysis* (Transaction, 1992), *Fraud and Fallible Judgment: Varieties of Deception in the Social and Behavioral Sciences* (Transaction, 1995), and *Tinder-Box Criminal Aggression: Neuropsychology, Demography, Phenomenology* (Transaction, 1996). Among his current research activities, he serves as the independent evaluation consultant to drug courts in the cities of Yonkers and Mount Vernon in Westchester County, New York.

Address correspondence to Dr. James J. Hennessy, Fordham University, 113 West Sixtieth Street, New York, NY 10023.

The "Drug Court Strengthening Families" Program

TK LOGAN

Center on Drug and Alcohol Research, University of Kentucky

CARL LEUKEFELD

Center on Drug and Alcohol Research, University of Kentucky

LISA MINTON

Kentucky Administrative Office of the Courts

JOANIE ABRAHMSON

Kentucky Administrative Office of the Courts

REBECCA HUGHES

Center on Drug and Alcohol Research, University of Kentucky

ABSTRACT Drug Courts were implemented in response to the rising incarceration rate of substance abusers. The Drug Court program is an intensive substance abuse treatment and criminal justice monitoring program. Children of Drug Court clients are at double risk–not only have their parents been substance abusers, they are also involved in the criminal justice system. This paper summarizes the results of a program needs assessment, process evaluation, and outcome evaluation of the Kentucky Drug Court Strengthening Families Pilot Program. Results indicated overall positive changes for families which resulted from the program. Several limitations and problems were identified and recommendations are offered for Drug

Court and other programs that target the children of substance abusers involved in the criminal justice system. The Kentucky Drug Court Strengthening Families Program provided an opportunity to prevent substance abuse for critically at-risk adolescents and pre-adolescents. *[Article copies available for a fee from The Haworth Document Delivery Service: 1-800-HAWORTH. E-mail address: <getinfo@haworthpressinc.com> Website: <http://www.HaworthPress.com> © 2001 by The Haworth Press, Inc. All rights reserved.]*

KEYWORDS At-risk children, drug court, family risk factors, family strengthening interventions, needs assessment, substance abuse prevention

At the end of 1996, more than 1.7 million adults were incarcerated, which represents a three fold increase in the number incarcerated from 15 years earlier (CASA, 1998). Much of this growth in the prison and jail population is due to drug law violators (Donziger, 1996). The U.S. Department of Justice Bureau of Justice Statistics indicated that at least 77%-81% of inmates were drug and/or alcohol abusers in their lifetime. Drug Court programs evolved in response to the overlap between drug/alcohol abuse and crime with efforts directed toward engaging defendants in substance abuse treatment (Blenko, 1998). The Drug Court is a court-managed drug intervention and treatment program designed to provide a cost-effective alternative to traditional criminal case processing (Blenko, 1998).

Drug Court programs are treatment-oriented and target clients whose major problems stem from substance abuse. There are three phases in the Kentucky Administrative Office of the Courts Drug Court program, which take an average of 18 months (see Logan et al., 2000 for a more complete description of a Kentucky Drug Court program). Phase I can be completed in one month. During the first phase clients are oriented to the program, begin treatment, are required to obtain court approved housing and employment, and begin sessions with the Judge. Phase II can be completed in eight months. Requirements in Phase II include continuing treatment, random urine screens, maintaining stable housing and employment, and performing other program requirements in a satisfactory manner. Phase III can be completed in three months and is typically referred to as the transitioning out phase. Requirements such as group attendance and random urine screens are decreased in this phase. Throughout the program, clients appear in Court regularly. Drug Court staff provide case notes for each client at court sessions. Although the Judge reviews written reports from the Drug Court staff, clients report directly to the Drug Court Judge in Court. The Drug Court Judge rewards success and sanctions noncompliance.

The children of Drug Court clients and other parents who are involved with both substance abuse and the criminal justice system are at high-risk for substance abuse and other risk factors, given their parent involvement in both substance abuse and the criminal justice system. This paper describes the evaluation results of a pilot substance abuse prevention program targeting the children of Drug Court clients. This information may be used as a guide to develop interventions for children of Drug Court clients as well as children of parents who are involved with substance abuse and/or the criminal justice system. The overall purpose of this paper is to present the results of a pilot program evaluation focused on children of Drug Court clients. Specifically, its goals are to (a) present the results of a needs assessment, (b) present the results of a process evaluation of the pilot Kentucky Drug Court Strengthening Families Program (SFP), and (c) present preliminary outcome evaluation findings for the pilot Kentucky Drug Court Strengthening Families Program.

PROGRAM NEED

High Risk Children: Children of Drug Court Clients

For adolescents, drug and alcohol abuse reduces motivation, interferes with cognitive processes, contributes to mood disorders, has implications for immediate and long-term physical health, and increases the risk of accidental injury or death (Hawkins, Catalano, & Miller, 1992; Paglia & Room, 1998). In addition, early substance use and abuse is associated with a variety of other risk factors including early and frequent sexual intercourse (which is associated with STDs, HIV, and unwanted pregnancies) as well as delinquency and later criminal activity (Ball et al., 1982; Dembo et al., 1991; Elliott, Huizinga, & Ageton, 1985; Jessor & Jessor, 1977; Speckhart & Anglin, 1985; Watters, Reinarmna, & Fagen, 1985). Precursors of drug and alcohol problems are described as risk factors. Risk factors have been associated statistically with an increased probability of drug abuse.

The family is one factor that appears consistently related to risk factors for drug abuse in the literature. Not only have family factors been directly associated with substance abuse, there is some evidence that family processes serve as mediators of peer selection (Conger & Rueter, 1996; Elliot, 1994; Kumpfer & Turner, 1990-1991). In general, family risk factors refer to family process/attachment/involvement that is typically defined as involvement with family, family communication, and discipline. Literature concerning family correlates of drug use indicate there are several aspects of the family that may contribute to the dissatisfaction of adolescents with their family as well as the initiation and continuation of substance use. Specifically, these family factors include family drug use, family composition, family conflict, family communication and discipline patterns, parent/child relations, family stress, and criminal justice involvement of parents (Adler & Lotecka, 1973; Gantman, 1978; Hamburg, Kraemer, & Jahnke, 1975; Hawkins, Catalano, & Miller, 1992; Kosterman et al., 2000; McCarthy & Anglin, 1990; Pandina & Schuele, 1983; Petraitis et al., 1998; Rees & Wilborn, 1983; Streit, Halsted, & Pascale, 1974; Tolone & Dermott, 1975; Wechsler & Thum, 1973).

Family drug use. Drug use by family members significantly increases the chance that other family members will also use drugs (Adler & Lotecka, 1973; Beardslee, Son, & Valliant, 1986; Blum, 1972; Craig & Brown, 1975; Denton & Kampfe, 1994; Needle, McCubbin, Wilson, Reineck, Lazar, & Mederer, 1986; Schuckit, 1992; Tec, 1974; Tolone & Dermott, 1975). Parents' behavior and attitudes toward substance use have also been significantly associated with the behavior and attitudes of their children (Adler & Lotecka, 1973; Cannon, 1976; Tec, 1974; Tolone & Dermott, 1975). In addition to modeling drug use, parents can influence adolescent and pre-adolescent drug use by modeling other behaviors, for example, by modeling antisocial values and behavior, failure to disapprove of drug use, failure to promote positive moral development, and neglecting to teach their kids life, social, and academic skills (Dielman et al., 1989; Grube & Morgan, 1986; Kandel & Andrews, 1987; Rutter, 1987; 1990).

Family composition. Family composition has a significant impact on adolescent substance abuse (Denton & Kampfe, 1994). For example, Kellam et al. (1983) reported identifying 76 different family structures and suggest that one of the best predictors of drug use among adolescents was a single-parent family with the mother as the parent. One-parent families and families with stepparents have been associated with increased risk of adolescent substance use, dependence, and need for illicit drug abuse treatment (SAMHSA, 1996). Family composition may contribute to adolescent drug use in several ways including poor supervision and neglect, which have been independently associated with drug use as well (Baumrind, 1985; Childcoat & Anthony, 1996; Garis, 1998; Jenkins & Zunguze, 1998; Johnson, Hoffman, & Gerstein, 1996; Loeber & Stouthammer-Loeber, 1986).

Family conflict. Several studies also indicate that children from broken homes, due to marital discord, are at higher risk for delinquency and drug use (Baumrind, 1985; Robins, 1980). Family conflict has been found to be a stronger predictor of delinquency than family structure (McCord, 1979; Rutter & Giller, 1983). Conflict has been associated with increased verbal, physical, or sexual abuse (Kumpfer & Bays, 1995; Kumpfer & DeMarsh, 1986). Family conflict has also been associated with learning poor conflict resolution or an-ger management skills, youth violence, associating with antisocial peers, and illicit drug use (Kumpfer & Turner, 1990-1991; Patterson, DeBaryshe, & Ramsey, 1989; Simcha-Fagan, Gersten, & Langner, 1986).

Communication and discipline patterns. Family characteristics associated with adolescent drug abuse include negative communication patterns; inconsistent, unclear behavior limits; and unrealistic parental expectations (Denton & Kampfe, 1994; Kosterman et al., 2000). Denton and Kampfe (1994) suggest that there is a communication gap between adolescents who are chemically dependent and other family members, which is supported by findings that adolescent drug abusers typically describe their parental communication as closed and unclear. Rigid communication patterns were also observed in these families. The literature also suggests that discipline is important in family interactions. For example, research has found that lax, inconsistent or harsh discipline, high levels of negative reinforcement, parental conflict over discipline practices, failure to set clear rules with consequences, unrealistic parental expectations for a child's developmental level, and excessive unrealistic demands or harsh physical punishment have been associated with drug use (Barnes, 1990; Barnes & Windle, 1987; Cohen & Brook, 1987; Jones & Houts, 1990; Kumpfer & DeMarsh, 1986).

Parent/child relations. Research indicates that parent/child relationships such as rejection of the child by the parents or of the parents by the child, low parental attachment, cold and unsupportive maternal behavior, lack of involvement and time together, and maladaptive parent/child interactions have all been associated with drug use (Baily & Hubbard, 1990; Baumrind, 1985; Brook et al., 1992; Kumpfer & DeMarsh, 1986; Kumpfer & Turner, 1990-1991; Newcomb, 1997; Newcomb, 1990; Ripple & Luthar, 1996; Shedler & Block, 1990). In fact, Reardon and Griffing (1983) suggest that positive child-parent association is vital to developing a strong self-concept and preventing drug abuse. For example, research has shown that the child-parent interaction contributes significantly to the level of adolescent drug use (Barnes, 1984; Barnes, Farrel, & Cairns, 1986; Dembo et al., 1985; Glynn, 1981; Johnson & Pandina, 1991; Tec, 1970; Vicary & Lerner, 1986). Other studies have reported that the lack of family cohesion and the lack of maternal involvement are related to drug initiation (Brook et al., 1992; Duncan, Duncan, & Hops, 1994). Sometimes children take on a parenting role for themselves and for their parents (Delgado, 1990; Szapocznik et al., 1986). Research indicates that some parents with drug-abusing adolescents view parenting as a job that requires suffering and sacrifice (Blum et al., 1972; Rees & Wilborn, 1983). These parents also reported a lack of confidence in child rearing. Further, research has shown that the effect of peers on delinquency and drug use is enhanced if parental attachment is low (Agnew, 1991; Hays & Revetto, 1990; Hundleby & Mercer, 1987).

Family stress. Risk factors related to family stress and chaos include poor family management skills, inadequate life skills, social isolation, and poverty (Bursik & Webb, 1982; Chassin et al., 1996; Farrington et al., 1986; Wolin, Bennett, & Noonan, 1979). Low family socioeconomic status has also been found to be associated with chronic delinquency and drug use in many studies (Farrington, 1991; Loeber & Dishion, 1983; Tracy, Wolfgang, & Figlio, 1990; Werner & Smith, 1992). Poor parental mental health including depression and irritability can cause negative views of the child's behaviors, parent hostility to the child, and harsh discipline (Conger & Rueter, 1996).

Family criminal justice system involvement. Parental deviance and instability may contribute to youth deviance by adversely affecting attachment, discipline, and supervision, thus increasing delinquency and drug use (Laub & Sampson, 1988; Sampson & Laub, 1994). Many of the same risk factors for drug use are risk factors for criminality. For example, Farrington et al. (1986) indicated that juvenile delinquents tended to come from large, poor families and/or families who were involved in the criminal justice system themselves; had families who were in conflict with each other; had families who were cruel, passive or neglecting; and/or had families who used harsh or erratic discipline. Other studies have reported that one of the most important predictors of whether or not a child will become a criminal is whether that child's father was a criminal (Reiss & Roth, 1993; Robins, 1979; Wilson & Herrnstein, 1985).

In summary, there are a number of risk factors that have been associated with substance use and abuse as well as related problem behaviors. Peer and family factors play a critical role in predicting substance initiation, use, and abuse. Family factors have also been shown to influence decisions about peers. The children of Drug Court clients are at increased risk for substance use and abuse. One of the most compelling reasons is that they are at double risk–not only have their parents been substance abusers, they also are involved in the criminal justice system. The consequences of parents being involved with both risk factors add even more to the number and type of risk factors their children must contend with, including: the impact on family composition, family conflict, family communication and discipline patterns, parent/child relations, and family stress. Thus, it is clearly established in the literature that there is a need to target children of Drug Court clients for substance abuse prevention; however, it is critically important to establish need at the local level.

Program Need–Local Level Results

Two sites were targeted for program implementation. The two Drug Court programs offer basic family counseling and referrals. However, there is no

Drug Court program funding to provide services to the high-risk children of Drug Court participants themselves.

Drug court client demographic background. That there are approximately 100 active clients at any one time in each of the two Drug Court Programs selected for the project (Logan et al., 2000; Logan, Leukefeld, & Williams, 1999a; 1999b). Clients were 70% male, half were African-American and half were White, and clients, on average, were 29 years old (18-52 years old). Approximately 64% of the clients had children, 30% were married, and 62% had never been married. Clients reported they had used drugs an average of 9 years, and about half had been in prior substance abuse treatment. Primary substances of choice were crack/cocaine, marijuana, and alcohol, although most of the clients had used a number of different kinds of drugs. In addition, clients had, on average, 5 prior charges and had spent approximately 10 months in jail before entering Drug Court. Clients had a history of the following kinds of charges: theft/property offenses, prescription drug fraud, drug possession, drug sales/trafficking (small quantities), parole/probation violations, and contempt of court charges. Approximately 40% of clients terminate from Drug Court in an average year.

Qualitative needs assessment. A qualitative needs assessment was conducted with Drug Court staff and clients. Both male and female parents expressed concern about parenting after years of substance abuse. Parents stated that they had lost the ability to parent, or realized that they never really were "effective" parents. The parents reported they now find themselves dealing with rebellious children, or children who had been accustomed to parenting themselves and their parents. Parents indicated they are unable to communicate with their children, and at times, do not feel respected by their children. They also stated that they did not have the skills needed to talk to their children about their past behaviors, their present situations, and their future goals for the family.

For example, one Drug Court graduate requested support from Drug Court staff because of problems she was having with her children. Her 23-year-old daughter had attempted suicide on the previous day; her 19-year-old son was incarcerated on two separate drug-related charges, one involved a shooting and the other involved a murder; and her youngest, a 14-year-old son, who was a good student who had no behavior problems, offended her by calling an addict on the street, a "crack head." She stated that he also used her past against her, and was very good at getting what he wanted from her by making her feel guilt and shame about her past drug using behavior. She asked not only for support, but also for advice and materials on how to maintain her sobriety and how to help her children. After spending some time with her, a staff member asked if she thought a family focused substance abuse prevention program would have been beneficial while she was in the Drug Court program. She emphatically replied "yes" and went on to explain how her addiction kept her from parenting for so many years, and now family communication and respect are difficult. She wanted to understand why her daughter did not come to her instead of trying to take her own life, why her son was involved in drugs when he saw where she was and all she went through, and why her younger son did not have any empathy toward those who are currently in the situation she was in a short time before.

Drug Court participants had children as young as 9 who were already deep into the juvenile justice system or in active addiction. Several of the parents have had children involved in both substance abuse inpatient and/or outpatient treatment programs. These situations enhanced the parents' feelings of guilt and shame and impacted their ability to concentrate on their own recovery. Many parents also had lost custody of their children to either relatives or the Cabinet for Families and Children, and wanted to regain custody. But there were problems for these parents in resolving issues with the Cabinet because of their long histories of substance abuse and previous non-compliance with treatment. Feelings of exasperation and confusion were expressed when trying to understand the system and their own children's behaviors.

Summary. Results suggest that the Drug Court families in both sites were drug users, included broken and single-parent families, had poor communication patterns, had poor discipline patterns, had high levels of conflict, had poor parent/child relationships, and had high levels of stress. Many of the parents had children involved in drug- and gang-related activities. Early family intervention and education is an effective tool in stopping the cycle of addiction and associated criminal behaviors. Drug Court program parents want to set good examples for their children and to be good parents. A family focused prevention program could provide a good foundation to build respect, open lines of communication, promote unity within families, and prevent substance abuse among their children.

PROCESS EVALUATION

Methods

Procedure

Face-to-face interviews were conducted with Drug Court Judges at both sites. The SFP coordinator and Drug Court program treatment coordinator at both sites were interviewed. Nine parents and 10 children who had completed the SFP were also surveyed about their perceptions of the program. Respondents were asked about program strengths and weaknesses as well as additional comments about specific aspects of the program including the curriculum, topics, activities, program length, and their impressions about the program effectiveness.

Results

Overview and Background

The Kentucky Drug Court SFP used the SFP model developed by Kumpfer, Molgaard, and Spoth (1994). The overall guiding principle of the SFP is that the family environment is an important factor in deterring the use of substances among youth. Family climate and parenting factors influence children's self-esteem. High self-esteem has been positively correlated with positive school bonding. Family environment is an important factor that influences even a child's choice of friends. Therefore, improving parent-child relationships is a major goal of the SFP. The SFP model also assumes that to reduce risk factors among children of substance abusers, it is necessary to improve the family environment and parents' abilities to provide appropriate opportunities for their children to receive rewards for positive attitudes and behaviors. The SFP has been extensively evaluated and has shown positive outcomes with substance abusing families as well as with low-income, rural, and urban African-American families, urban Hispanic/Latino families, and rural and urban Asian and Pacific Island families in particular (Kumpfer, Molgaard, & Spoth, 1996; NIDA, 1997a; 1997b). Specifically, the program has been effective in achieving its goals and reducing: (a) family environmental risk factors; (b) behavioral and psychological risk factors for substance abuse among the children; (c) tobacco and alcohol use in children who had initiated use; and (d) intentions to use tobacco, alcohol and other drugs in the future for the children. For the parents, outcomes of the SFP were: (a) dramatic reduction in depression; (b) reduced substance abuse, and (c) improved parenting skills. In addition, a five-year follow-up study at several sites found that parents reported the SFP made a dramatic difference in their children's behavior, improved the parent-child relationship and communication, and reduced family conflict (Harrison, 1994; Kumpfer, Molgaard, & Spoth, 1996; NIDA, 1997).

Kentucky Drug Court SFP Description

The Drug Court Strengthening Families Program (SFP) had 21 parents and 34 children graduate from the program. The program began in November 1998 and ended June 2000. During this time span, three cohorts completed the program in each site.

Drug Court families participated in the program after they entered Phase II of the Drug Court program. Drug Court clients, if they qualified for the program, were mandated to participate in the program by the Drug Court Judge. There were no fees for SFP participation. Clients and children met once a week for two hours at the Drug Court site. Specifically, the Strengthening Families Program (SFP) was designed to reduce family environmental risk factors and improve protective factors with the ultimate goal of increasing the resiliency of youth who are at risk for substance abuse. There are three components to the weekly meetings: parent skills training, children's skills training, and family skills training. During the first hour of the weekly sessions, parents and children attend separate sessions. The second hour is scheduled with the families together.

The parent session of the SFP was presented through a variety of teaching methods including lectures, demonstrations, discussions, role-plays, homework assignments, practice exercises, and video presentations. The curriculum focused on developmental expectancies, stress management, communication, reward systems, appreciation, problem solving, discipline, drugs/alcohol, and family values. Parents met as a group with the program coordinator to learn about and discuss these issues and how each pertains to their own families. Parents openly discussed what their families were experiencing and the problems they faced day-to-day. Feedback from other parents and the group leader provided new and different ways to overcome these problems. Parents also learned ways to improve their relationships and interactions with other family members.

The youth component consisted of similar issues. Curriculum topics covered social skills, communication, respect, appreciation, stress management, good behavior, drug/alcohol use and abuse, problem solving, coping skills and resources to obtain further help if needed. Each session incorporated varied teaching methods to increase interest and encourage learning. Active learning techniques such as games, role-plays, making visuals, demonstrations, and other projects as well as through lectures and group discussions provided alternative ways for youth to learn. Youth learned not only from the curriculum, but also from the other youths in their group. In these sessions youth met others with similar life experiences. Through self-disclosing discussions with one another, youth learned they were not alone and could learn from others' experiences as well.

The SFP family component brought the youths and their parents together to discuss issues concerning the entire family. Families met in a group with the group leader to discuss topics including family values, problem solving skills, respect, appreciation, alcohol/drug use, and reward systems. Families practiced holding family meetings and practiced solving family conflict and other problems. Parents and youth also participated in role-playing where youths played the role of parent and parents played the role of the youth. This aided better understanding of the other family members' views. Projects and games were incorporated into the family sessions to encourage the importance of spending quality time together. Family homework assignments included setting goals for the week such as holding a family meeting and setting aside specific times to play games and talk with one another.

Four adaptations were made to the original SFP specifically for Drug Court clients and their children. First, for this project, the age range for child participants was expanded to 8-15 years of age. If a child's age upon entering the program was slightly above or below the set age range that determined eligibility (e.g., the child would be 8 years old the next month) he or she participated in the program. Second, a criminal justice component was added to one of the youth sessions. In this session, a law official such as a Drug Court Judge and/or police officer met with the youth to discuss their jobs and the legal system and to take part in games and activities with the youth. This component was added to give youth a chance to form a positive relationship with law officials and to understand what their Drug Court parent might be experiencing. Third, one family outing was added to the program for each cohort, such as a pizza party, bowling, or skating event. This family outing was incorporated to encourage families to spend recreational time together. Fourth, an eighth session was added to review and conclude the program. During the final session, families reviewed the material they had learned in the previous seven sessions. Questions and games with points or snacks awarded to those with the correct answers were used to facilitate review. After the review, families concluded the program with a celebration. These celebrations consisted of a pizza party or other snacks and refreshments, free discussion, and games and/or other activities.

Eligibility. The Drug Court Judge and case specialists worked together with the Strengthening Families Program Coordinator to recruit eligible clients. In order to be eligible for the program, Drug Court clients had to (a) be in Phase II of the Drug Court program; and (b) have at least one child between the ages of 8-15. When clients were determined to be eligible for the SFP, the Drug Court Judge mandated attendance and participation in all sessions as part of the client's Drug Court obligations. If the client did not comply with the Judge's requirement and missed a session, then a client was given a sanction. Drug Court clients in Phase III of the Drug Court program were not eligible for the Strengthening Families program because they may have become eligible for graduation from Drug Court before the Strengthening Families program could have been completed.

Respondent Perceptions

Judge and staff perceptions. Judges and staff agreed that the Strengthening Families Program provided Drug Court clients and their children with an opportunity to obtain a structured neutral meeting ground to discuss difficult issues such as family substance abuse. Parents were also given a chance to regain their parenting role and regain the respect of their children. Communication and respect among family members was one of the most important program components perceived by staff and Judges. Involving the entire family allowed those most affected by the substance abuse to help in the treatment process.

Parent perceptions. Parents who successfully completed the Strengthening Families Program agreed during the structured meetings that the program impacted their lives. Parents involved in the program reported that the program gave them an opportunity to discuss their addiction problems more openly with their family and to gain knowledge about how it affected their partners and children. It also allowed for an opportunity to discuss problems associated with drugs and opened the door for other family topics such as loss of respect for one another or unhealthy communication between family members. Parents also reported that the program taught them better ways to communicate with their children and new ways to discipline. They also learned how important it was to respect their children and spend quality time with them. Several parents reported that the program allowed them to spend more time with their children and actually get to know their children. Parents, when asked what they learned in the program, reported that they learned better ways to communicate with their children, to respect their children, and new ways to discipline "that really worked."

Child perceptions. Children reported that the program taught them not to use drugs and how to moderate peer pressure. It also helped the children to get closer to their parents, work out family problems, learn how to better express themselves and communicate with their families, and also how to make their families what they wanted. Many children also stated that the program provided an opportunity to meet similar families, which helped them feel not so alone. Children reported that their favorite parts of the program were playing games and doing family projects because they got to interact with their families and others.

Limitations

Drug Court Judges and staff agreed that one major program limitation was locating Drug Court clients that fit eligibility requirements. Eligible clients who did not have full custody of their children were required to try to make arrangements with the custodial parent so their child/children could participate in the program. Some custodial parents refused to allow a Drug Court parent to have any contact with the child/children, making that potential participant no longer eligible for the program. In other cases, children were involved in extra curricular activities that conflicted with the program meetings and were unable to attend. This also made a potential Drug Court participant ineligible. Joint custody also provided a problem if meetings were held on days the Drug Court client did not have visitation. The other parent sometimes did not allow a child to participate because it conflicted with their visitation time. Some of the clients who participated in the program dropped out because they lost custody of their child/children during the program and/or the other parent refused to let the children attend after they started the program. Families also dropped out of the program if the Drug Court parent failed to fulfill his or her obligations to Drug Court, resulting in a sanction during the program, or if the client was terminated from Drug Court.

Process Evaluation Summary

The SFP is a scientifically developed prevention intervention program adapted to specifically target Drug Court clients and their children ages 8-15. The eight-week program incorporated three separate sessions for youth, parents, and families (youths and parents together). Participants learned ways to improve family cohesiveness, communication skills, substance use prevention skills, listening skills, discipline approaches, coping skills, and problem solving which included activities such as games, projects, role-playing, discussions, writing assignments, demonstrations, practice exercises, and video presentations. The primary goals of the program included: (a) reducing the use of alcohol, tobacco, and other drugs; (b) delaying the initial use of alcohol, tobacco, and other drugs; (c) decreasing the positive attitudes toward alcohol, tobacco, and other drugs; and (d) lowering significant family risk factors. Evaluation results indicate that this program is effective in modifying family functioning and substance abuse prevention. The adaptations facilitated program implementation specifically for the Drug Court target population.

Qualitative results suggest the SFP was effective for Drug Court clients and their children who participated and successfully completed the program. Most participants agreed that some of the highlights of the program included (a) the family day outing; (b) family projects; and (c) games. These activities provided families with an opportunity to take time out to actually be a family and spend quality time together. Children also learned peer pressure resistance skills. Although locating and maintaining eligible families was an unexpected complication, those families that did complete the program described it as a bonding experience.

OUTCOME EVALUATION

Methods

Participants

The two groups of outcome evaluation participants were (a) Drug Court parents and their children who participated in the Strengthening Families Program; and (b) a control group of parents and children who did not participate in the Strengthening Families program. Overall, 30 children completed the Drug Court Strengthening Families Program with pretest and posttest interviews. The average age was 11; the majority of the children were white, and 60% were female. Overall, 19 parents completed the Strengthening Families Program with pretest and posttest interviews. The average parent age was 36, 53% were white, and 42% were female. Ten of the parents had one child in the program, 8 parents had two children, and 1 parent had four children in the program. There were 8 control children with an average age of 11, and 50% were female. There was a total of 8 control parents with an average age of 34 years, and 57% were female.

Materials

Parent and child program participants were interviewed separately prior to the first SFP session and immediately after the last SFP session. Parents and children were also administered a follow-up interview six months after completing the SFP. Each interview lasted about 35 minutes. Parent interviews included family questions, information about their child's drug use, school bonding, their child's self-esteem, behavior, feelings toward their child, personality characteristics present in their child, and their own self-esteem and personality characteristics. Child interviews incorporated questions about their family, friends, self-esteem, personality characteristics, attitudes and behavior concerning drugs, and knowledge about drugs. Control participants were also administered the same interviews during the same timeframes as the program participants. Measures were adapted from the original SFP evaluation (Kumpfer, Molgaard, & Sopoth, 1996), as well as from other adolescent questionnaires (Achenbach & Edelbrock, 1983; Loeber et al., 1998; 1999a; 1999b; Lynam et al., 1999; Sulik & Lynam, 1997).

Procedure

The SFP intervention was implemented every six months across both Drug Court program sites. The program data for this report were for the period November 1998 through June 2000. Three cohorts completed the SFP in each site. For each of the families who participated in the SFP intervention, data were collected three times. The three data collection points were: baseline data collection, post-program data collection, and a 6-month follow-up.

Baseline. Once eligibility was established, pretest interviews were scheduled with each participant. Participants were interviewed individually and confidentially at each Drug Court site. Before each interview, the interviewer briefly overviewed the study and the nature of the interview. Both control and experimental parents were asked to sign a consent form allowing for both themselves and their child/children to be interviewed. A copy of the consent form was also given to the parent. Parents were interviewed about each child participating in the program. Each child was asked to sign an assent form before being interviewed.

Follow-up interviews. Immediately after the eight-week program was completed, interviews were scheduled with all the participants and the control group. Six-month follow-ups were administered to parents and children who participated in the SFP and who were in the control group. Follow-up interviews adhered to the same procedures as baseline interviews. Participants were consented and interviewed individually and confidentially.

Control group. Because the children of families involved in a Drug Court program are at such high risk and because the intervention had never been applied to a Drug Court population, a control group was utilized. There was only one control group. The control group was recruited at the same time as the first program cohort and was recruited from Drug Court clients and graduates who had children in the same age range (8-15 year olds) as the program group, but who were not eligible to participate in the SFP intervention because: (a) the Drug Court client parent was in Phase III of the program; or (b) the Drug Court program client had recently graduated. Analysis revealed there were no significant differences between control and program parents and children.

Analysis

Analysis of Variance (ANOVA) and chi-square analysis were used to examine differences between groups. Because of the low number of parents and children that completed pretests and posttests, site comparisons were not made.

Results

Drop-Out Rates

Overall, 55 parents and children completed the Strengthening Families Program, and 30 dropped out of the program. There was a 38% drop-out rate for children, and a 39% drop-out rate for parents. Both children and parents who completed the program were similar to the children and parents who dropped out of the program on age, race, and gender. Attrition from the SFP was associated with parent termination from the Drug Court program. There were also a number of parents who were not able to bring the child to the program either because the other parent would not allow the child to participate or because the children moved too far away to be able to participate. In addition, there were 2 control children and 5 control parents who dropped out from baseline to follow-up. Demographic comparisons showed no significant differences between control completers and control dropouts.

Baseline Characteristics for Youth Who Completed the Program

Overall, 30 youths completed the Drug Court Strengthening Families Program with both pretest and posttest interviews. Twelve children ranged in age from 7-10 years old, of whom 9 were girls. Nine youths, of whom 5 were girls, were 11-13 years old, and 9 children were 14-16 years old, of whom 4 were girls.

Selected family contact and interaction. Table 1 shows selected parental contact and interaction by age group. In 60% of the families, the father was the Drug Court program client. Eighty-three percent saw their Drug Court parent at least weekly (50% daily), and 75% saw their non-Drug Court parent at least weekly (57% daily). Forty-two percent of the youngest age group and 33% of the middle age group reported they had trouble "getting along" with their parents compared to the older age group.

Table 1 also displays selected children's self-reported feelings by age group. Forty-four percent of the children in the middle age group reported feeling angry at home most of the time or always compared to 17% of the youngest age group and 11% of the oldest age group. Almost 60% of all three groups reported they do not tell their fathers when they are feeling angry or sad, and 40% reported they do not tell their mothers when they are feeling angry or sad.

Table 1 also shows selected school performance indicators. Almost 80% of the middle age group and half of the youngest age group reported asking someone to help them with their homework the week preceding the interview. Sixty-seven percent of the middle age group and 42% of the youngest age

Table 1: Baseline Child Demographics and Family Situation

	7-10 years old (n = 12)	11-13 years old (n = 9)	14-16 years old (n = 9)	Total (n = 30)
% Father was the Drug Court client	58	78	44	60
% See Drug Court parent once or twice a week	33	11	22	23
% See non-Drug Court parent once or twice a week	25	22	0	17
% Mom did not even say once she loved them	17	11	0	10
% Dad did not even say once he loved them	25	22	22	23
% Did not talk to mom about stuff they were interested in	50	22	11	30
% Did not talk to dad about stuff they were interested in	17	33	22	23
% Had trouble getting along with their parents	42	33	78*	50
% Feel angry at home most of the time or always	17	44	11	23
% Do not tell mother when they are sad	50	11	56	40
% Do not tell father when they are sad	67	44	56	57
% Asked for help with homework last week	50	78	11*	47
% Mother helped with homework last week	42	67	0*	37
% Mom usually or always helps with homework when asked	67	89	33	63
% Dad usually or always helps with homework when asked	75	56	11*	50
% Always finish their homework	42	78	22	47
% Involved in extracurricular activities	75	89	44	70
% DC parent involvement in extracurricular activities is very little or not at all	42	56	33	43

*p < .05

group reported that their mothers helped them with their homework in the previous week compared to none of the oldest age group. Seventy-five percent of the youngest age group, 56% of the middle age group, and 11% of the oldest age group reported that their fathers helped them with homework most of the time or always when they asked for help. Overall, 70% of the children reported being involved in extracurricular activities, but 43% reported their Drug Court parent was involved in their extracurricular activities very little or not at all.

Friends. Table 2 shows selected indicators of friends' problem behaviors in the previous three months by age groups. Thirty-seven percent of these children had at least two friends who had skipped school one or more times in the preceding 3 months. Seventy-eight percent of the oldest age group had two or more friends who had skipped school compared to only 17% of the youngest

Table 2: Baseline Child Friend Behavior and Child Substance Use and Problem Behavior				
	7-10 years old (n = 12)	11-13 years old (n = 9)	14-16 years old (n = 9)	Total (n = 30)
% Had 2 or more friends skip school	17	22	78**	37
% Had 2 or more friends damage or destroy property	8	11	44*	20
% Had 2 or more friends steal something worth more than $100	17	0	11	10
% Had at least one or more friends attack someone with a weapon	8	44	11	20
% Had friends who smoked cigarettes	25	44	89	50
% Had friends who used alcohol	8	0	56*	20
% Had friends who used marijuana	0	11	67*	23
% Had friends who lied, defied, or talked back to an adult	58	78	78	70
% Had friends who took a motor vehicle for a ride without the owner's permission	0	11	44	17
% Had friends who bullied others to get something	8	22	11	13
% Had 2 or more friends who hit someone with the intent to hurt that person	17	44	67	40
% Ever smoked cigarettes	17	78	67*	50
% Smoked cigarettes in the past 30 days	0	0	45	13
% Ever used alcohol	25	56	67	47
% Drank at least one full glass of alcohol	0	11	44*	17
% Used alcohol in the past 30 days	0	0	11	3
% Ever used marijuana	0	0	56**	17
% Used marijuana in the past 30 days	0	0	11	3
% Skipped school	8	11	11	10
% Lied or talked back to an adult	50	89	67*	67
% Damaged or destroyed property	8	22	0	10
% Hit someone with the intent to hurt them	33	33	67	43
% Attacked someone with a weapon	8	0	22	10
% Took a motor vehicle for a ride without the owner's permission	0	0	11	3
% Stole something worth less than $5	25	11	22	20

*p < .05 **p < .01

age group and 22% of the middle age group who had friends that skipped school. Forty-four percent of the oldest age group had at least two friends who had damaged or destroyed someone else's property compared to only 8% of the youngest age group children and 11% of the middle age group having reported the same about their friends.

Fifty percent of the children reported they had friends who smoked cigarettes, showing a gradual increase with age progression. Over half of the oldest age group had friends who used alcohol and marijuana in the previous three months. Both the youngest age group and the middle age group reported very little use of these substances among their friends when compared to the use of these substances by the friends of the children in the oldest age group. Increases in friends' problem behaviors as age progresses were also reported as shown in Table 2.

Substance use. Table 2 also shows the children's drug use by age group. The middle age group reported the most cigarette use (78%) compared to 67% among the oldest group and only 17% of the youngest group. Sixty-seven percent of the oldest age group children reported using alcohol compared to 56% of the middle age group children and 25% of the youngest age group children. Forty-four percent of the oldest group and 11% of the middle group reported drinking at least one full glass of alcohol. The oldest group also reported the highest marijuana use with a total of 56% compared to none of the children in either the middle or youngest groups. The average age of first cigarette and first alcohol use was 8 years old with no significant differences by age group. Only the oldest group reported ever trying marijuana and reported first trying marijuana at 13 years old.

Problem behaviors. Table 2 shows selected problem behaviors for the three age groups. Overall, 67% reported they had lied or talked back to an adult on at least one occasion in the previous three months; however, the middle and older groups reported lying or talking back significantly more than the younger group. Thirty-three percent of the youngest and middle age groups, and 67% of the oldest group had hit someone with the intent to hurt that person at least one time in the previous three months. One-fourth of the youngest age group reported stealing something that was worth less than five dollars in the previous three months compared to 11% of the middle age group and 22% of the oldest age group.

In summary, these children had contact with both their Drug Court parent and their non-Drug Court parent. Most of these children lived with their mothers while their fathers were more often Drug Court clients. Reported problem behaviors of friends increased as age increased. Reported problem behaviors of the program youths also increased with age. In fact, as suggested in the literature, children in this program had similar or higher substance use rates than national estimates (Johnston, O'Malley, & Bachman, 1999a; 1999b). Baseline data suggest that these children are at risk for both substance use and delinquency, and it is critical to provide these children with substance abuse prevention, and their parents with parenting skills enhancement.

Parent Baseline Data

Overall, 19 parents completed the Strengthening Families Program with pretest and posttest interviews. Table 3 displays parents' perceptions of their youngest child and their second to the youngest child who were in the SFP. Both the youngest and the next to the youngest child were an average age of 11 years old (both ranged from 8 to 15 years of age).

Family contact and interaction. Table 3 shows the majority of the SFP parents reported seeing their children daily or at least once a week. Fifty-three percent reported their youngest child lived with them, and 56% indicated their

Table 3: Baseline Parent Demographics and Family Situation

	Youngest (n = 19)	Next Youngest (n = 9)
% See child everyday	53	56
% See child at least weekly	74	89
% See other parent daily	58	67
% See other parent at least weekly	84	89
% Child lives with biological mother	58	67
% Child lives with biological father	37	44
% Child lives with Drug Court parent	53	56
% Reported other parent was in the child's home or the local area	84	89
% Child has behavior problems at home	58	89
% Never had trouble getting along with their child	58	33
% Praised their child two times or less	37	22
% Talked once or not at all with their child about stuff they were interested in	32	11
% Reported doing something special with child only once or not at all	58	67
% Child involved in at least one extracurricular activity	68	44
% Reported they were involved very little or not at all in their child's extracurricular activity	42	100
% Reported their child was left alone at home at least two hours a day	37	44
% Did not know the name of their child's teacher	74	89
% Child had at least one academic difficulty	53	67
% Child had behavior problems in school	63	67
In the last 3 months		
% Child had bullied another child	48	44
% Child had initiated physical fights	42	22
% Child had engaged in physically dangerous activities	53	55

next youngest child lived with them. Table 3 shows parental involvement in their children's extracurricular activities. The majority of the youngest children were involved in extracurricular activities such as band/choir, sports/dance, and/or clubs and also hobbies such as collecting coins, toys, etc. Most parents were involved in their younger children's activities, with only 42% reporting they were involved very little or not at all in their youngest children's extracurricular activities. However, parents reported less involvement in their older children's activities.

School performance. Selected indicators of school performance are displayed in Table 3. Seventy-four percent of the parents did not know the name of their younger child's teacher, and 89% of the parents did not know the name of their older child's teacher. A little over half of the parents reported their younger child and 67% reported their older child had academic difficulties in school.

Problem behaviors. Table 3 shows the children's problem behaviors as reported by their parents in the preceding three months. Over half of all the parents reported their children have engaged in activities that were physically dangerous (53% and 55%). Forty-eight percent of the parents reported that their younger child, and 44% reported their older child bullied other children. Further, 42% of the parents reported their youngest child initiated a physical fight on at least one occasion.

Substance use. Parents were asked how many days in the past month their children used substances including cigarettes, smokeless tobacco, alcohol, marijuana, solvents, pep pills, painkillers, cocaine, Ritalin for hyperactivity, and codeine cough syrups. Specifically, only one parent knew his or her younger child had smoked cigarettes in the past month. There were no other reports of the youngest children using drugs of any kind. Parents did report substance use for the older children. Twenty-two percent reported their older children had smoked cigarettes; 11% of the parents reported their older children drank alcohol; and 11% reported their older children used pep pills in the preceding month.

Pre/Post Differences Between Program and Control Children

There were few significant differences between program and control children from baseline to follow up, in part because of the small sample size. Table 4 shows the adjusted means. The program increased positive interaction with parents. Although the means were not significantly different, they were in the general direction. Program involved youth were less likely to have skipped school in the preceding three months at follow up ($F(1,33) = 6.3$, $p < .10$) and were more likely to report talking with their dads about "stuff" they were inter-

Table 4: Significant Pre/Post Differences for Children and Parents

CHILDREN	PROGRAM (N = 30)	CONTROL (N = 8)
# Times skipped school	0	.73***
# Times talked to dad about stuff they were interested in	2.1	.62*
# Times mom helped with homework	3.8	3.2
# Times dad helped with homework	3.4	2.6
# Times mom said something positive	3.2	1.4
# Times dad said something positive	3.3	3.3
Get sad often	2.3	1.7**
Fight with other kids	.77	0**
Will not drink alcohol when older	.5	1.2**
PARENTS	PROGRAM (N = 19)	CONTROL (N = 8)
How often do you have trouble getting along with child	1.2 (Once or twice a day)	2.4 (once or twice a week)*
Talk about stuff child is interested in	3.4 times	2.2 times***
Child drank alcohol past 30 days	0 times	.37 times**

*$p < .05$ **$p < .10$ ***$p < .20$

ested in at follow up ($F(1,24) = 2.0$, $p < .20$) than control children. In addition, program children reported they were sad less often than control children ($F(1,34) = 3.6$, $p < .10$) and were less likely to report they would drink alcohol when they got older than control children ($F(1,32) = 2.9$, $p < .10$). Program children were, however, slightly more likely to report fighting with other children at follow-up than control children ($F(1,34) = 2.8$, $p < .10$).

Pre/Post Differences Between Program and Control Parents

There were very few significant differences between program and control parents from baseline to follow-up. Parents in the program reported talking to their children about their interests more often than control parents ($F(1,34) = 2.2$ $p < .20$). Program parents also reported that their children drank alcohol less than control parents reported ($F1,36) = 3.0$, $p < .10$). Program parents, however, reported more trouble getting along with their children at follow up than control parents ($F(1,37) = 7.5$, $p < .01$).

Six-Month Follow-Up Perceptions of SFP

Follow-up interviews were conducted with program parents and children approximately six months after completion of the Strengthening Families Program. A total of 7 program parent follow-up interviews and 11 program child follow-up interviews were conducted. Follow-up interviews were also conducted with 7 control parents and 7 control children. There were no significant differences at the 6-month follow up for problem behavior or substance use on either child or parent reports. However, results of the six-month follow up need to be interpreted with caution because of the low number of follow-up interviews conducted.

Qualitative perceptions of the program at six-month follow up indicated positive changes six months after graduation. Children reported that the program taught them not to use drugs. Youth participants stated they learned family values, life lessons, and peer pressure resistance skills. The youths reported that they learned to respect their parents, to be nice to others, and to be a leader and not a follower. The youth also reported that they learned better ways to deal with stress and their emotions and also how to think about potential consequences before they act or behave in a certain manner.

The program parents thought the best thing about the SFP was becoming closer to their child/children by participating in the family activities like games, family projects, and the family day outing. Many parents mentioned that the staff of the SFP was very understanding and supportive. Program parents also said they enjoyed meeting other families who were in similar situations. When asked what they learned in the SFP, parents reported that they learned better ways to communicate with their children and different ways to discipline. Parents stated the new ways of discipline helped them set limits and show love at the same time. Many parents reported that they learned a reward system that has proven to be very effective in their homes. Parents stated that they learned not only that their children must show them respect, but also that they must show respect to their children and acknowledge their opinions and feelings. Parents also stated they learned that constantly yelling and criticizing their children was not effective and that having a positive attitude was important.

Discussion

In summary, the qualitative results of the program were very positive, indicating that both parents and children who completed the SFP learned communication skills, peer pressure resistance skills, and family relations skills. In addition, the children indicated that learning about substance use was important and helpful. Positive views of the program were maintained over time for the families that participated in the 6-month follow up. Results indicated trends toward improved family functioning, decreased child problem behavior, and decreased substance use for program families compared to control families.

There were several major contributing factors to the lack of significant results that are more related to the characteristics of the program evaluation than to the program. First, implementation of the Strengthening Families Program was originally intended for three Drug Court sites. However, not only was the program not implemented at all in one site, there were fewer program and control participants than originally anticipated at the two implementation sites. A small number of participants in each group limits statistical power (Lipsey, 1990). Limiting the statistical power can increase Type II error (Cook & Campbell, 1979). Type II error occurs when there are true differences between the groups, but significance cannot be determined due to low power. In addition to the small number of participants who were eligible and able to participate, there was a 40% drop-out rate. This drop-out rate parallels the drop-out rates for the Drug Court program in general (Logan et al., 2000; Logan, Leukefeld, & Williams, 1999a; 1999b). Providing payment to both program and control group participants may have increased the post and follow-up rates. Finally, it is possible that the parents and children underreported drug use, problem behavior, and family functioning due to fear of punishment from the criminal justice system and/or from the parents for the children. This would cause minimal variance from baseline to follow up regardless of whether or not there was change.

Regardless of these limitations, this study provides important information about programs targeting children of Drug Court clients and other families involved in substance abuse and the criminal justice system. Preliminary data from this pilot suggest that it is important to continue to provide services to these high-risk children. This pilot project provided information about what can be done to improve program success. One improvement is related to family recruitment. Spending time with each prospective family including the custodial parent and step-parent to personally answer questions and concerns, may facilitate program participation. This could include home visits to the other parents and step-parents. In addition, involving families who are not in the Drug Court program (e.g., targeting parents on probation) could increase SFP participation rates. If Drug Court families were not completely spotlighted they may feel less pressure to report their families in a positive light. It is also possible that Drug Court parents and children underreported behaviors given the overlap of Drug Court program staff and Strengthening Families Program staff. It is important that both program staff and evaluators of prevention programs targeting this kind of population are completely separated from the primary target agency. Finally, providing compensation for baseline and follow-up interviews could ensure better follow-up participation rates for both the program families and the control families.

Clearly more research is needed to focus on substance abuse prevention for children of substance abusing parents involved in the criminal justice system. More evaluation research examining both short-term and long-term effects of prevention programs is needed. In addition, research to examine family engagement and completion rates for these kinds of programs would also be important. Finally, researching strategies for maintaining behavior change and/or abstinence from substance use for these children is important.

In summary, the research literature, the needs assessment, the process evaluation, and the baseline data all indicate that children of Drug Court clients should be targeted for substance abuse prevention interventions. In addition, Drug Court families need strong science-based interventions to help provide more stable and effective homes for the children. Although the qualitative information from this study was positive and there were some trends toward significance, indicating positive results for the quantitative data, there were several limitations to this study including the small number of participants and high rates of attrition in the control and experimental groups, as well as the possible underreporting of problem behaviors on the part of the parents as well as the children. Several recommendations are offered, including increasing family recruitment efforts, hiring staff that are independent of the Drug Court program, and increasing funding for the evaluation efforts. In conclusion, the program met a significant need for some of the most high-risk children. The children of Drug Court clients are at double risk–not only have their parents been substance abusers, they are also involved in the criminal justice system. The Drug Court Strengthening Families Program provided an opportunity to make a real difference with regard to preventing substance abuse for at-risk adolescents and pre-adolescents.

REFERENCES

Achenbach, T. & Edelbrock, C. (1983). *Child Behavior Checklist (CBCL)*. University Medical Education Associates, Inc., 1 South Prospect Street, Burlington, VT 05401-3456.

Adler, P. & Lotecka, L. (1973). Drug use among high school students: Patterns and correlates. *The International Journal of Addictions, 8(3)*, 537-548.

Agnew, R. (1991). The interactive effects of peer variables on delinquency. *Criminology, 29*, 47-72.

Bailey, S. & Hubbard, R. (1990). Developmental variation in the context of marijuana initiation among adolescents. *Journal of Health and Social Behavior, 31*, 58-70.

Ball, J., Rosen, L., Flueck, J., & Nurco, D. (1982). Lifetime criminality of heroin addicted in the United States. *Journal of Drug Issues, 12*, 225-239.

Barnes, G. & Windle, M. (1987). Family factors in adolescent alcohol and drug abuse. *Pediatrician, 14*, 13-18.

Barnes, G. (1990). Impact of the family on adolescent drinking patterns. In R. Collins, K. Leonard, & J. Searels (Eds.), *Alcohol and the family: Research and clinical perspectives.* (pp. 137-162). New York: Guilford.

Barnes, G.M. (1984). Adolescent alcohol abuse and other problem behaviors: Their relationships and common parental influences. *Journal of Youth and Adolescence, 13*, 329-348.

Barnes, G.M., Farrel, M.P., & Cairns, A. (1986). Parental socialization factors and adolescent drinking behaviors. *Journal of Marriage and the Family, 48*, 27-36.

Baumrind, D. (1985). Specious causal attributions in the social sciences: The reformulated steppingstone theory of heroin use, an exemplar. *Journal of Personality and Social Psychology, 45*, 1289-1298.

Beardslee, W., Son, L. & Vaillant, G. (1986). Exposure to parental alcoholism during childhood and outcome in adulthood: A prospective longitudinal study. *British Journal of Psychiatry, 149*, 584-591.

Blenko, S. (1998). *Research on drug courts: A critical review.* The National Center on Addiction and Substance Abuse at Columbia University. New York: Columbia University.

Blum, R. (1972). White middle-class families. In W.E. Henry, & N. Sanford (Eds.), *Horatio Alger's Children* (pp. 65-94). London: Jossey-Bass.

Brook, J.S., Cohen, P., Whiteman, M. & Gordon, A.S. (1992). Psychosocial risk factors in the transition from moderate to heavy use or abuse of drugs. In Glantz, M.D. and Pickens, R.W. (Eds.), *Vulnerability to Drug Abuse.* (pp. 359-388). Washington, DC: American Psychological Association Press.

Bursik, R. & Webb, J. (1982). Community change and patterns of delinquency. *American Journal of Sociology, 88*, 24-42.

Cannon, S. (1976). *Social functioning patterns of families of offspring receiving treatment for drug abuse.* New York: Libra.

CASA. (1998). *Behind Bars: Substance Abuse and America's Prison Population.* The National Center on Addiction and Substance Abuse at Columbia University. New York: Columbia University.

Chassin, L., Curran, P., Hussong, A., & Colder, C. (1996). The relation of parent alcoholism to adolescent substance use: A longitudinal follow-up study. *Journal of Abnormal Psychology, 105*, 1, 70-80.

Chilcoat, H. & Anthony, J. (1996). Impact of parent monitoring on initiation of drug use through late childhood. *Journal of the American Academy of Child and Adolescent Psychiatry, 35*, 1, 91-100.

Cohen, P. & Brook, J. (1987). Family factors related to the persistence of psychopathology in childhood and adolescence. *Psychiatry, 50*, 332-345.

Conger, R. & Rueter, M. (1996). Siblings, parents, and peers: A longitudinal study of social influences in adolescent risk for alcohol use and abuse. In G. Brody (Ed.),

Sibling relationships: Their causes and consequences. Advances in applied developmental psychology. (pp. 1-30). Norwood, NJ: Ablex.

Cook, T. & Campbell, D. (1979). *Quasi-experimentation: Design & analysis issues for field setting.* Boston, MA: Houghton Mifflin Company.

Craig, S. & Brown, B. (1975). Comparison of youthful heroin users and nonusers from one urban community. *The International Journal of the Addictions, 10*, 53-64.

Delgado, M. (1990). Hispanic adolescents and substance abuse: Implications for research treatment and prevention. In A. Stifman & L. Davis (Eds.), *Ethnic Issues in Adolescent Mental Health.* (pp. 303-320). Newbury Park, CA: Sage.

Dembo, R. Grandon, G., Taylor, R.W., La Voie, L., Burgos, W. & Schmeidler, J. (1985). The influence of family relationships on marijuana use among a sample of inner city youth. *Deviant Behavior, 6*, 267-286.

Dembo, R., Rarrow, D., Schmeidler, J., & Burgos, W. (1991). Testing a causal model of environmental influence on early drug involvement of inner city junior high school youths. *American Journal of Drug and Alcohol Abuse, 6*, 313-336.

Denton, R. & Kampfe, C. (1994). The relationship between family variables and adolescent substance abuse: A literature review. *Adolescence, 29*, pp. 475-495.

Dielman, T., Shope, J., Leech, S., & Butchart, A. (1989). Differential effectiveness of an elementary school-based alcohol misuse prevention program by type of prior drinking experience. *Journal of School Health, 59*, 255-263.

Donzinger, S. (1996). *The real war on crime: The report of the national criminal justice commission.* Harper-Perennial: New York.

Duncan, T., Duncan, S., & Hops, H. (1994). The effects of family cohesiveness and peer encouragement on the development of adolescent alcohol use: A cohort-sequential approach to the analysis of longitudinal data. *Journal of Studies on Alcohol, 55*, 588-599.

Elliot, D. (1994). Health enhancing and health compromising lifestyles. In S. Millstein, Petersen, & Nightingale (Eds.). *Promoting the health of adolescents: New directions for the twenty-first century.* New York: Oxford University Press.

Elliott, D., Huizinga, D. & Ageton, S. (1985). *Explaining delinquency and drug use.* Beverly Hills, CA: Sage.

Farrington, D. et al. (1986). Unemployment, school leaving, and crime. *British Journal of Criminology, 26*, 335-356.

Farrington, D. (1991). Childhood aggression and adult violence: Early precursors and later life outcomes. In D. Pepler & K. Rubin (Eds.), *The development and treatment of childhood aggression.* (pp. 5-29). Hilsdale, NJ: Lawrence Erlbaum.

Gantman, C. (1978). Family interaction patterns among families with normal, disturbed, and drug-abusing adolescents. *Journal of Youth and Adolescence, 7*, 429-440.

Garis, D. (1998). Poverty, single-parent households, and youth at-risk behavior: An empirical study. *Journal of Economic Issues, 32*, 4, 1079-1085.

Glynn, T.J. (1981). From family to peer: A review of transitions of influence among drug-using youth. *Journal of Youth and Adolescence, 10*, 363-383.

Grube, J. & Morgan, M. (1986). *Smoking, drinking, and other drug use among Dublin post-primary school pupils.* Dublin: Economic and Social Research Institute.

Hamburg, B., Kraemer, H., & Jahnke, W. (1975). A hierarchy of drug use in adolescence: Behavioral and attitudinal correlates of substantial drug use. *American Journal of Psychiatry, 132,* 1155-1163.

Hawkins, J.D., Catalano, R.F., & Miller, J.Y. (1992). Risk and protective factors for alcohol and other drug problems in adolescence and early adulthood: Implications for substance abuse prevention. *Psychological Bulletin, 112,* 64-105.

Hays, R. & Revetto, J. (1990). Peer cluster theory and adolescent drug use: A reanalysis. *Journal of Drug Education, 20,* 191-198.

Hundleby, J. & Mercer, G. (1987). Family and friends as social environments and their relationship to young adolescents' use of alcohol, tobacco, and marijuana. *Journal of Marriage and the Family, 49,* 151-164.

Jenkins, J., & Zunguze, S. (1998). The relationship of family structure to adolescent drug use, peer affiliation and perception of peer acceptance of drug use. *Adolescence, 33,* 132, 811-813.

Jessor, R.R. & Jessor, S. (1977). *Problem behavior and psychosocial development: A longitudinal study of youth.* San Diego, CA: Academic Press.

Johnson, L., O'Malley, P., & Bachman, J. (1999a). *Cigarette smoking among American teens continues gradual decline.* University of Michigan News and Information Services: Ann Arbor, MI. Available: www.monitoringthefuture.org.

Johnson, L., O'Malley, P., & Bachman, J. (1999b). *Drug trends in 1999 are mixed.* University of Michigan News and Information Services: Ann Arbor, MI. Available: www.monitoringthefuture.org.

Johnson, R. Hoffman, J., & Gerstein, D. (1996). *The relationship between family structure and adolescent substance use.* Substance Abuse and Mental Health Services, Department of Health and Human Services. Washington: DC.

Johnson, V. & Pandina, R.J. (1991). Effects of the family environment on adolescent substance use, delinquency, and coping styles. *American Journal of Drug and Alcohol Abuse, 17,* 71-88.

Jones, D. & Houts, R. (1990). Parental drinking, parent-child communication, and social skills in young adults. *Journal of Studies on Alcohol, 53,* 48-56.

Kandel, D. & Andrews, K. (1987). Processes of adolescent socialization by parents and peers. *International Journal of the Addictions, 22,* 319-342.

Kellam, S.G., Brown, C., Rubin, B., & Ensminger, M. (1983). *Paths leading to teenage psychiatric symptoms and substance abuse: Developmental epidemiological studies in Woodlawn.* In S. Guze, F. Earls, & J. Barrett (Eds.), *Childhood psychopathology and development.* (pp. 17-51). New York: Raven.

Kosterman, R., Hawkins, D., Guo, J., Catalano, R., & Abbott, R. (2000). The dynamics of alcohol and marijuana initiation: Patterns and predictors of first use in adolescents. *American Journal of Public Health, 90,* 3, 360-366.

Kumpfer, K. & Bayes, J. (1995). Child abuse and alcohol, tobacco, and other drug abuse: Causality, coincidence, or controversy? In J. Jaffe (Ed.), *The Encyclopedia of Drugs and Alcohol.* (Volume I, pp. 217-222). New York: Simon & Schuster.

Kumpfer, K. & DeMarsh, J. (1986). Family environmental and genetic influence on children's future chemical dependency. In Griswold-Ezekoye, Kumpfer, & Bukoski (Eds.), *Childhood and chemical abuse; Prevention and intervention.* (pp. 49-91). New York: The Haworth Press, Inc.

Kumpfer, K. & Turner, C. (1990-1991). The social ecology model of adolescent substance abuse: Implications for prevention. *International Journal of the Addictions*, 25, 435-463.

Kumpfer, K. (1994). *Strengthening America's families: Promising parenting and family strategies for delinquency prevention: Users Guide*. Office of Juvenile Justice and Delinquency Prevention, U.S. Department of Justice Grant No 87-JS-CX-K495). Silver Spring, MD: Aspen Systems.

Kumpfer, K., DeMarsh, J., & Child, W. (1989). *Strengthening families program: Children's skills training curriculum manual, parent training manual, children's skills training manual, and family skills training manual*. Salt Lake City: University of Utah, Social Research Institute, Graduate School of Social Work.

Kumpfer, K., Molgaard, V., & Spoth, R. (1996). Family interventions for the prevention of delinquency and drug use in special populations. In R. Peters & R. McMahon (Eds.), *Preventing childhood disorders, substance abuse, and delinquency*. (pp. 241-265). Thousand Oaks: Sage.

Laub, J. & Sampson, R. (1988). Unraveling families and delinquency: A re-analysis of the Gluecks' data. *Criminology*, 26, 355-380.

Lipsey, M. (1990). *Design sensitivity: Statistical power for experimental research*. Newbury Park, CA: SAGE.

Loeber, R., & Dishion, T. (1983). Early predictors of male delinquency: A review. *Psychological Bulletin*, 94, 68-99.

Loeber, R., Farrington, D., Stouthammer-Loeber, M., Moffitt, T., & Caspi, A. (1998). The development of male offending: Key findings from the first decade of the Pittsburgh Youth Study. *Studies on Crime and Crime Prevention*, 7, 2, 141-171.

Loeber, R., & Southammer-Loeber, M. (1986). Family factors as correlates and predictors of juvenile conduct problems and delinquency. In N. Morris & Tonry (Eds.) *Crime and justice: An annual review of research*. Chicago: University of Chicago Press.

Loeber, R., Stouthammer-Loeber, M., & White, H. (1999a). Developmental aspects of delinquency and internalizing problems and their association with persistent juvenile substance use between ages 7 and 18. *Journal of Clinical Child Psychology*, 28, 3, 322-332.

Loeber, R., Wei, E., Stouthammer-Loeber, M., Huizanga, D., & Thornberry, T. (1999b). Behavioral antecedents to serious and violent offending: Joint analysis from the Denver Youth Survey, Pittsburgh youth study and the Rochester youth development study. *Studies on Crime and Crime Prevention*, 8, 2, 245-263.

Logan, T., Leukefeld, C., & Williams, K. (1999a). *Fayette Drug Court process evaluation*. Center on Drug and Alcohol Research, University of Kentucky.

Logan, T., Williams, K., & Leukefeld, C. (1999b). *Warren Drug Court process evaluation*. Center on Drug and Alcohol Research, University of Kentucky.

Logan, T., Williams, K., Leukefeld, C., & Minton, L. (2000). A process evaluation of a Drug Court: Methodology and results. *International Journal of Offender Therapy and Comparative Criminology*, 44, 3, 369-394.

Lynam, D., Milich, R., Zimmerman, R., Novack, S., Logan, T., Martin, C., Leukefeld, C., & Clayton, R. (1999). Project DARE demonstrates no effects at ten-year follow-up. *Journal of Consulting and Clinical Psychology*, 67, 4, 590-593.

McCarthy, W. & Anglin, M. (1990). Narcotics addicts: Effect of family and parental risk factors on timing of emancipation, drug use onset, preaddiction incarcerations, and educational achievement. *Journal of Drug Issues, 20*, 99-123.

McCord, J. (1979). Some child-rearing antecedents of criminal behavior in adult men. *Journal of Personality and Social Psychology, 37*, 1477-1486.

Molgaard, V. (1999). *Strengthening families across the lifespan.* http://www.exnet.iastate.edu/Pages/families/sfpeval.html.

National Institute on Drug Abuse. (1997). *Drug abuse prevention for at-risk groups.* (NIH Publication No. 97-4114). Rockville, MD.

National Institute on Drug Abuse. (1997). *Drug abuse prevention: What works.* (NIH Publication No. 97-4110). Rockville, MD.

Needle, R., McCubbin, H., Wilson, M., Reineck, R., Lazar, A. & Mederer, H. (1986). Interpersonal influences in adolescent drug use–the role of older siblings, parents, and peers. *The International Journal of the Addictions, 21*, 739-766.

Newcomb, M. (1990). Social support by many other names: Toward a unified conceptualization. *Journal of Social and Personal Relationships, 7*, 479-494.

Newcomb, M. (1997). General deviance and psychological distress: Impact of family support/bonding over 12 years from adolescence to adulthood. *Criminal Behavior and Mental Health, 7*, 369-400.

Paglia, A. & Room, R. (1998). Preventing substance use problems among youth: A literature review and recommendations. *ARF Research Document Series #142.* Toronto: Addiction Research Foundation.

Pandina, R. & Schuele, J. (1983). Psychosocial correlates of alcohol and drug use of adolescent students and adolescents in treatment. *Journal of Studies on Alcohol, 44*, 950-973.

Patterson, G., DeBaryshe, B., & Ramsey, E. (1989). A developmental perspective on antisocial behavior. *American Psychologist, 44*, 329-335.

Petraitis, J., Flay, B., Miller, T., Torpy, E., & Greiner, B. (1998). Illicit substance use among adolescents: A matrix of prospective predictors. *Substance Use and Misuse, 33*, 13, 2561-2604.

Reardon, B. & Griffin, P. (1983). Factors related to the self-concept of institutionalized, white, male, adolescent drug abusers. *Adolescence, 18*, 29-41.

Rees, C. & Wilborn, B. (1983). Correlates of drug abuse in adolescents: A comparison of families of drug abusers with families of nondrug users. *Journal of Youth and Adolescents, 12*, 55-63.

Reiss, A. & Roth, J. (1993). *Understanding and preventing violence.* Washington, D.C.: National Academy Press.

Ripple, C. & Luthar, S. (1996). Familial factors in illicit drug abuse: An interdisciplinary perspective. *American Journal of Drug and Alcohol Abuse, 22*, 147-172.

Robins, L. (1979). Sturdy childhood predictors of adult anti-social behavior: Replications from longitudinal studies. *Psychological Medicine, 8*, 611-622.

Robins, L. (1980). The natural history of drug abuse. *Acta Psychiatrica Scandinavia, 62*, 7-20.

Rutter, M. & Giller, H. (1983). *Juvenile delinquency: Trends and perspectives.* New York: Guilford Press.

Rutter, M. (1987). Continuities and discontinuities from infancy. In J. Rolf, Masten, Cicchettie, Neuchterlein, & Weintraub (Eds.), *Risk and protective factors in the development of psychopathology.* New York: Cambridge University Press.

Rutter, M. (1990). Psychosocial resilience and protective mechanisms. *American Orthopsychiatric Association*, 316-331.

SAMHSA (1996). *The relationship between family structure and adolescent substance use.* U.S. Department of Health and Human Services. Washington: DC.

Sampson, R. & Laub, J. (1994). Urban poverty and the family context of delinquency: A look at structures and process in a classic study. *Child Development*, *65*, 523-540.

Schuckit, M. (1992). A clinical model of genetic influences in alcohol dependence. *Journal of Studies on Alcohol*, *55*, 5-17.

Shedler, J. & Block, J. (1990). Adolescent drug use and psychological health: A longitudinal inquiry. *American Psychologist*, *45*, 5, 612-630.

Simcha-Fagan, O., Gersten, J. & Langner, T. (1986). Early precursors and concurrent correlates of items of illicit drug use in adolescence. *Journal of Drug Issues*, *60*, 7-28.

Speckart, G. & Anglin, M. (1985). Narcotics use and crime: An analysis of existing evidence for a causal relationship. *Behavioral Science and the Law*, *3*, 259-283.

Streit, F., Halsted, D. & Pascale, P. (1974). Differences among youthful users and non-users of drugs based on their perceptions of parental behavior. *The International Journal of the Addictions*, *9*, 749-755.

Sulik, R. & Lynam, D. (1997). Survey of adolescent problems and strengths (SOAPS). The Departments of Psychiatry and Pediatrics and Department of Psychology, University of Kentucky.

Szapocznik, J. et al. (1986). Bicultural effectiveness training: An intervention modality for families experiencing intergenerational/intercultural conflict. *Hispanic Journal of Behavioral Sciences*, *6*, 3093-330.

Tec, N. (1974). Parent-child drug abuse: Generational continuity or adolescent deviancy? *Adolescence*, *4*, 351-364.

Tolone, W. & Dermott, D. (1975). Some correlates of drug use among high school youth in a midwestern rural community. *The International Journal of the Addictions*, *10*, 761-777.

Tracy, P., Wolfgang, M. & Figlio, R. (1990). *Delinquency careers in two birth cohorts.* New York: Plenum Press.

Vicary, J.R. & Lerner, J.V. (1986). Parental attributes and adolescent drug use. *Journal of Adolescence*, *9*, 115-122.

Watters, J., Reinarmna, C., & Fagan, J. (1985). Causality, context, and contingency relationships between drug abuse and delinquency. *Contemporary Drug Problems*, *12*, 351-373.

Wechsler, H. & Thum, D. (1973). Teen-age drinking, drug use, and social correlates. *Quarterly Journal of Studies on Alcohol*, *34*, 1220-1227.

Werner, E. & Smith, R. (1992). *Overcoming the odds: High-risk children from birth to adulthood.* Ithaca, NY; Cornell University Press.

Wilson, J. & Herrnstein, R. (1985). *Crime and Human Nature.* New York: Simon and Schuster.

Wolin, S., Bennett, L., & Noonan, D. (1979). Family rituals and the recurrence of alcoholism over generations. *American Journal of Psychiatry*, *136*, 589-593.

AUTHORS' NOTES

TK Logan, PhD, is currently an assistant professor in the Department of Psychiatry at the University of Kentucky, Center on Drug and Alcohol Research. Dr. Logan has been funded by the National Institute on Drug Abuse (NIDA) to examine the nature, extent, and co-occurrence of HIV risk behavior, victimization, and drug use among crack users and by the National Institute on Alcohol Abuse and Alcoholism (NIAAA) to study alcohol, violence, mental health and health status and utilization among rural and urban women with protective orders. Dr. Logan has conducted over 20 process evaluations of different Drug Court programs across the state of Kentucky. Dr. Logan is currently conducting outcome evaluations for three Kentucky Drug Court sites. Dr. Logan has conducted a statewide Drug Court needs assessment and currently is developing a Drug Court statewide Management Information System. Dr. Logan also currently serves as a co-principal investigator on two NIDA funded studies focused on criminal justice populations and on the Kentucky Treatment Outcome Study. Dr. Logan's primary interests are in the area of violence, health and mental health issues, substance use, and HIV risk behavior.

Carl Leukefeld, DSW, is a professor of Psychiatry and Behavioral Science at the University of Kentucky, and the Director of the Center on Drug and Alcohol Research. He has given numerous presentations and written articles focused on treatment, criminal justice, prevention, and AIDS. He has co-edited and written thirteen books and monographs and has over fifty published articles and chapters. He is an editor or consulting editor for four professional journals and has served as a consultant to several international and national organizations including the Council on Europe, World Health Organization, several European countries, US Customs, US Army, US Navy, Administrative Office of the US Courts, National Institute of Justice, National Institute of Corrections, American Probation and Parole Association, as well as state and local agencies. He is a Kentucky Colonel and is the former Chief Health Services Officer, United Public Health Service.

Lisa Minton was appointed manager of the Drug Courts division of the Administrative Office of the Courts (AOC) when the division was established July 1, 1996. Prior to that, she was a field supervisor for Pretrial Services, an AOC statewide program. She has also managed an adult literacy program and taught GED classes in rural Kentucky. She oversees Kentucky's 10 operational adult and 5 operational juvenile sites; 21 pilot/planned adult and 11 pilot/planned juvenile sites; and one planned family drug court site. The Fayette and Jefferson Drug Courts are National Mentor training sites. Ms. Minton has been a speaker at a wide array of state and national training sessions and has co-authored several publications on Kentucky's drug courts.

Joanie Abrahmson is employed by the Kentucky Administrative Office of the Courts as the Field Manager for the Drug Courts division. She has over 20 years experience in various leadership, administrative, supervisory, and research capacities within the criminal justice system. Skills and experiences include: directing a statewide drug court program; statistical compilation; special reports; project/grant management; curriculum development; developing printed materials; conference and program planning; research; legislative tracking; parole board, 2 terms; counseling and rehabilitation of medical and criminal clientele. She has a Master of Arts degree in Counseling Psychology and also Psychological Assessment.

Rebecca Hughes, at the time of this writing, was a student at the University of Kentucky. She graduated in May 2001 with a bachelor's degree in psychology. She plans to continue her education in graduate school with a focus in clinical psychology and pursue her career as a child and family psychologist. In her spare time she enjoys reading and traveling.

This study was funded by the Kentucky Administrative Office of the Courts and the Department of Mental Health and Mental Retardation Services, Division of Substance Abuse, Kentucky Incentive Program Grant # 1UIFSPO8109-01.

Address correspondence to Dr. TK Logan, Center on Drug and Alcohol Research, University of Kentucky, 643 Maxwelton Court, Lexington, KY 40506-0350.

Issues of Race and Gender in Court-Ordered Substance Abuse Treatment

ADELA BECKERMAN

Nova Southeastern University

LEONARD FONTANA

Broward Community College

ABSTRACT In the last decade Drug Courts have been developed in hundreds of American communities. Little attention in the research has been given to the retention of diverse client groups who have been subject to legal inducement for treatment through Drug Courts. This article examines a Drug Court that offered culturally specific programming as a strategy to enhance retention in the treatment of female and African-American male substance abuse offenders. The study found that mandating treatment is insufficient to foster client engagement. Retention was significantly enhanced by treatment that recognized cultural differences among client populations. *[Article copies available for a fee from The Haworth Document Delivery Service: 1-800-HAWORTH. E-mail address: <getinfo@haworthpressinc.com> Website: <http://www.HaworthPress.com> © 2001 by The Haworth Press, Inc. All rights reserved.]*

KEYWORDS Drug court, gender, race, drug treatment, alternatives to incarceration, substance abuse, criminal offender

During the last four decades the problem of drug use has had a significant impact on the criminal justice system. The segment of society using drugs during the 1950s through 1980s grew dramatically with the widespread use of heroin, marijuana, and different forms of cocaine. Early efforts to reverse this development centered on redefining criminal codes and enacting stiffer penalties for drug possession and sales. While these actions had little impact on reducing drug use, they did manage to fill American prisons. An unanticipated consequence of the resulting overcrowding of prisons with drug offenders was the compromise in the criminal justice system's ability to respond to violent and career felons. Subsequent efforts to "build out" of the problem by constructing new correctional facilities strained state budgets to the point where alternatives to mandatory incarceration of drug offenders were sought. It was in this context that the interest of communities in "drug courts" developed.

The widespread development of Drug Courts in the 1990s challenged many traditional beliefs and practices regarding substance abuse and criminal behavior. The traditional adversarial system was seen as being counter productive to the treatment of offenders with alcohol or drug addictions, since the "defense" of the offender often involved the denial of a substance abuse problem. Furthermore, if convicted, there was ambivalence about assessing offenders as to their need for treatment. Typically, if any form of treatment was provided, it was limited and not provided until long after the arrest. The practice of releasing or placing first time offenders on probation also undermined any serious efforts to reduce continued drug use. If referrals to treatment did take place, which was not very often, it would often take months for treatment to begin, with little or no legal inducement to complete the treatment.

The hallmark of the Drug Court is the combination of criminal justice sanctions with drug treatment–often described as "therapeutic jurisprudence." The premise of the Drug Court treatment program is that the threat of being incarcerated serves as a stimulant to engage and retain clients in treatment. Treatment completion typically results in setting aside any felony sentence for the drug offense. In contrast, persistent use of substances, one example of treatment "failure," prompts a change in status–the client is terminated from treatment and is sentenced by the Drug Court.

There have been efforts in the past to rehabilitate drug abusers involved in criminal activities using a "compulsory treatment" format. The literature, however, is not consistently positive in finding that clients mandated for treatment have better treatment outcomes than other clients (Leukefeld & Tims, 1988). Studies of diversion programs in operation in the 1970s and 1980s, such as Treatment Alternatives to Street Crime (TASC) and the California Civil Addict Program, found generally positive outcomes. The data, for example, indicate that "compulsory treatment" clients often stayed in treatment much longer than voluntary clients, a finding which is usually associated with better treatment outcomes. There is a question, however, as to whether the relationship between compulsory treatment and positive outcomes is universal for all groups of clients. Duvall et al. (1963), in an early study, noted the limitations of coercive treatment when comparing black males who had been in treatment voluntarily, with black prisoners. Maddux (1988) stressed the limitations of external coercion. He noted that erratic personality and behavioral traits of drug users easily compromise treatment impact, and that positive treatment results are limited if follow up monitoring is not extensive.

The impact of the treatment program for mandated clients can also be obviated by the attitude of "going along with the program." As Maddux noted, while coercion may bring a person into a program, it cannot force that person to become engaged. Limited data collection and program monitoring efforts have restricted the information and conclusions that can be culled from these earlier research efforts. The development of the Drug Court "movement" offers an opportunity to closely examine the attributes and benefits of compulsory treatment for drug-involved criminal offenders.

There are more than 400 Drug Courts in the United States today representing a variety of models for alternatives to incarceration that can be found in the more than 400 drug courts in operation in the United States currently. While research indicates promising outcomes (Belenko, 1998; Platt et al., 1998), it has been generally acknowledged that there is a need for research to establish the relative effectiveness of the different program features being utilized to treat drug offenders within the context of legal inducement. The research discussed in this study was shaped and formed by a number of gaps in what we know about Drug Courts. The focus of the study is on "retention" of clients in a Drug Court, since the substance abuse treatment literature is clear that retention is one of the key predictors of positive treatment outcomes. Treatment outcomes improve in proportion to the amount of time spent in drug abuse treatment. This pattern has been found to persist regardless of the specific type of treatment modality (Leukefeld and Tims, 1990; Simpson, 1988).

The fairly recent introduction of Drug Courts has not been accompanied by an aggressive research agenda to evaluate its impact on program participants. Researchers have yet to achieve an informed assessment of the strategies that enhance the retention and impact of Drug Court treatment. In particular, little attention has been given in the research literature to assessments of the impact of strategies that enhance retention for diverse client populations. Racial identity and gender, for example, are relatively ignored in the Drug Court research literature. This article examines a Drug Court treatment program that offered enhanced programming targeted toward the needs of its diverse client population. Accordingly, the focus of the study was on program variables related to the retention of two distinct client populations–female and African-American male clients in a Drug Court program.

ENHANCED SERVICES TO DIVERSE CLIENT GROUPS

The Drug Court program that is the focus of this research is located in South Florida. The program began in the early 1990s, and was one of the earliest Drug Courts in the United States. At the onset, anecdotal accounts from counselors indicated the need to recognize gender and race in the court-mandated treatment of drug offenders (Terry, 1993, 1999). An examination of those arrested for drug charges in the service area of the Drug Court found that about 82 percent were male. The disproportionate number of males arrested for drug offenses persisted regardless of the drugs involved. The persons arrested were also disproportionately African-American, far exceeding their representation in the local population.

While only 15 percent of the local population was African-American, 46 percent of those arrested on drug charges were African-American. The types of drug offenses for racial groups differed as well. While two-thirds of those arrested for marijuana use were Caucasian, only 33 percent were African-American. The reverse was true for those charged with cocaine offenses. Sixty-four percent of those arrested were African-American, while only 36 percent were Caucasian. The patterns of drug use and the associated criminal behavior of the male and female drug offenders admitted to the Drug Court program were noticeably different as well. Different treatment approaches for men and women, and for Caucasian and African-American males appeared to be warranted.

The Drug Court judges as well as treatment staff observed that accumulated evidence suggested that drug use progressed differently and had different consequences for male and female program participants. Recognizing this, the Drug Court program in South Florida attempted to respond to the unique challenges posed by two subsets of its client population. With the assistance of a grant, a distinctive culturally specific enhancement strategy was developed to serve female and African-American male Drug Court clients.

African-American male clients. Addiction professionals have come to realize that powerful cultural and social factors have an impact on addictive behaviors, and the effectiveness of treatments offered to remedy those behaviors. Treatment effectiveness, it is argued, is clearly related to the provider's knowledge of the client's culture, and to the degree to which interventions are synchronous with that culture's traditions (Atkinson and Lowe, 1995; Sue, Arredondo, and McDavis, 1992). DeLeon et al. (1993), for example, found that the absence of a culturally appropriate treatment approach contributed to the disproportionately low retention of African-American clients in therapeutic community programs.

Bell and Evans (1981) and Amuleru-Marshall (1993) found that African-American clients often resist seeing substance abuse as a primary causal factor of the problems they encounter in their lives. Addictions are seen as secondary to the causal factors of racism and poverty. This contradicts most standard treatment protocols, which view substance abuse as the primary disease that requires initial attention for recovery to occur. Bell and Evans argue that to be effective with African-American clients, treatment programs must take into account the special circumstances of, and acknowledge the omnipresent impact of, race in society.

Numerous features need consideration in the development of culturally specific treatment strategies for working with African-American male Drug Court clients. Brisbane (1992) called attention to the stigma that is often present if any form of treatment is perceived as "mental health" treatment. Terrell and Terrell (1984) also found that African-American clients' resistance to mental health counseling is related to the race of the counselor and the presence of "cultural" mistrust. Treatment features, such as the manner in which intervention is delivered and the "language and verbal expressions" used by addictions professionals, may be troubling to clients.

Treatment protocols that utilize mixed-gender group intervention strategies are questioned when serving an African-American male client population. Vontress (1995) argued that the experiences of African-American males are distinctive and unique. He pointed to the societal obstacles to be a provider for one's family and community, and the dominant role that women often play in the socialization of children. Vontress recommended the use of single-gender groups in which treatment staff can address drug use and associated issues, such as the developmental experience of African-American males, without the inhibitions present in mixed-gender groupings.

Female clients. There is a paucity of research on the treatment of female substance abusers. Most studies have focused on males, and the studies that address females are often dominated by concerns about pregnant women. The research that is available stresses the need for programs to attend to the cultural context of the female clients' addictions. Women differ from men in their worldview, priorities, values, and approach to relationships (Carter, 1991). Drug Court counselors need to be attuned to the cultural dynamics of the female addict's life experiences. Treatment "failures" often occur if the primary focus of treatment is on abstinence from drugs, without recognition of the context of gender socialization and gender-specific experiences.

The literature stresses the importance of treatment that is sensitive to the cultural experiences of females, and of treatment providers who are culturally competent (Lewis, 1994). Attention to the role of relationships with spouses, partners, and children, as well as other relatives, is central. Female addictions are often associated with a long history of emotional and sexual victimization and resultant self-denigrating behaviors and sense of powerlessness. Mejta (1982), for example, argued that women's use of substance abuse typically occurs within the context of their relationship with men. Women are often introduced to substance abuse and associated legal activities through such relationships.

Research encourages single-gender treatment opportunities. Issues that concern male-female relationships may be difficult to process in mixed-gender settings. Males often dominate the style and content of programming as a result of their disproportionately large numbers in treatment programs, and their style of interacting. The diverse styles commonly used by female participants are overshadowed. As a result, the benefits that should accrue to female participants are impeded (Hodgins, El-Guebaly, and Addington, 1997). Females/women also tend to respond to treatment approaches differently than males/men. Confrontation, for example, seems to be less effective for women (Covington, 1998). The employment of single-gender treatment regimens for women that foster collaborative relationships that are respectful and safe are thus encouraged (Mejta, 1982).

Case management functions. Female and African-American male substance abusers often face multiple chronic problems that "feed" their substance abuse. The presence of unemployment, homelessness, unstable living conditions, inadequate or non existent financial resources and health problems are common factors that aggravate and diffuse efforts to arrest addictive behaviors among these client groups. The ecological nature of addictions suggests that retention and treatment completion would be encouraged by case management services (Wilenbring et al., 1991; Loneck, Garrett, and Banks, 1997).

Studies of case management in substance abuse treatment programs have found multiple, interrelated benefits. Brokering to access housing, medical care, parenting classes and other services were found to significantly increase retention and attainment of treatment goals (McLellan et al., 1999). In a study of four treatment modalities, Schwartz et al. (1997) found that case-managed clients were more likely to remain in treatment and achieve treatment outcomes than clients who received no case management assistance. Case managers complemented the work of addictions counselors, mastering the array of community resources and services that enhanced efforts to address clients' co-existing problems (Mejta, Bokos, and Mickenberg, 1997).

ENHANCEMENT PROGRAM DESIGN AND COMPONENTS

The design for the enhanced Drug Court treatment program developed in South Florida differed substantially from the regular treatment regimen. The latter revolved around large, heterogeneous group meetings that were didactic in style, and offered limited opportunity for interaction. The "enhancement" program offered a different format, consisting of small single-gender group sessions for females and for African-American males. Opportunities for extensive contact and interaction between counselors and clients outside of group sessions were provided. Assessment of client need for support services and resources was accompanied by the brokering of services with and for program participants. Case management services were integral.

The "enhancement" program was dedicated to Drug Court clients who were not making progress in the regular treatment program. Clients who presented a complexity of problems and exhibited a recalcitrant attitude and behavior toward the expectations of the Drug Court program were referred to the "enhancement" program.

The cultural and political context within which clients view their addictions provided the framework for the treatment design of the enhanced treatment program. The issues addressed in group sessions were far-reaching. In the African-American male group sessions, the role of the male in the family and community, the nature of spiritual growth, and the need to master core life skills related to enhancing employability were examined. Particular attention was also given to dissecting the presence of a "counterculture of selling" among substance abusers in the local community.

The females' single-gender group sessions acknowledged developmental and societal factors that prompt and foster feelings of powerlessness and low self-worth. While the group sessions explored means of correcting and arresting addictive behaviors, they also emphasized the shared nature of the group members' experiences. The group sought to diminish the perception of individual members being "at fault," refocusing participants' energies in constructive directions. An emphasis was placed on identifying, applauding, and maximizing the strengths and capabilities of participants.

Two Drug Court addiction counselors were dedicated to the specialized "enhancement" program. Both had competence in the approach being utilized, and were adept at tailoring their "helping style" to the cultural context of program participants. The role of these addictions counselors was expansive. Each assumed responsibility for facilitating group meetings with either female or African-American male clients as well as case management with that client group. A vocational rehabilitation counselor supported the counselors, conducting assessments of educational and employment capabilities, and referring clients for appropriate educational and employment opportunities.

Comprehensive case management of client needs and ongoing monitoring of client progress were integral components of the Drug Court's "enhancement" program. When assessments indicated the need for more comprehensive treatment and support services than could be provided directly by the program staff, referrals were made. Assessments and referrals incorporated sensitivity to the cultural context of client's addictive behaviors. Affiliations between the "enhancement" program and other public and private service providers were established, and a broad range of services were available. These included detoxification services, transportation and housing assistance, health care, and vocational/educational services. "Success" in reaching treatment goals was perceived as being partially dependent on participants' access to, and ability to utilize, support services, both during and following treatment. This was seen as being essential to clients' developing the sense of empowerment needed to live substance and crime-free lives.

RESEARCH DESIGN

The research focus was on the impact of the enhancement strategies on the retention of female and African-American male clients in the Drug Court treatment program. The research examined whether the enhancement strategies were effective in retaining the types of female and African-American male clients who, in the past, had absconded or withdrawn from the Drug Court program. Were the female and African-American male clients in the "enhancement" program more likely to attend the treatment program than their counterparts in the regular Drug Court treatment program?

Two measures of effectiveness were utilized. The results of urinalysis tests administered to participants served as an indicator of abstinence, and the length of time participants remained in treatment served as a measure of retention. These two measures of effectiveness have a logical and intuitive appeal. If participants in the enhancement program were more invested in the program's ability to assist in their recovery and forestall incarceration than their non-enhancement program counterparts, one would expect to observe more persistence in the program over time and improvement in the number of negative urinalysis test results among "enhancement" group members.

An experimental group was identified as the population of clients who began treatment in the "enhancement" program during the first nine months of the program's inception. The experimental group consisted of 57 clients, 24 females and 33 African-American males. The treatment staff provided the research team with computer printouts of data on salient features and program participation of each client and their program participation. Urinalysis test results and the length of time that the client had remained in the program thus far were included.

Since the aim of the research was to ascertain any increase in retention as a result of the specialized services offered in the "enhancement" program, a "comparison group" was identified. The comparison group consisted of females and African-American males who had been in the Drug Court treatment program during the nine-month period prior to the introduction of the "enhancement" program. The comparison group consisted of females and African-American males who met the criteria for inclusion in the "enhancement" program–they were recalcitrant, noncompliant and uncooperative. They would have been referred to the "enhancement" program, had it been in operation at that time. A total of 56 clients, 26 females and 30 African-American males were included in the comparison group.

DATA ANALYSIS

Female clients. A comparison of the experimental and the comparison female client groups indicated no significant differences in terms of their age, employment status, or level of education at the time of their admission to the Drug Court (see Table 1). The average age of the experimental group women was 37; the average age of the comparison group women was 33.

Table 1 also presents the drugs commonly reported at intake. Significant differences were not found between drugs reported by the women in the two groups studied. Polysubstance use was evident. Cocaine/crack was one of the drugs of choice identified by most women in both the experimental (75%) and comparison (62%) groups. Marijuana/hashish and alcohol were also prominent as drugs of choice. Few women in either group reported using heroin.

Prior arrest information was not available for the women in the experimental group but data were available for 24 of the 26 women in the comparison group. The data indicated that 54% had been arrested once before, 38% had been arrested at least twice before, and 8% had no prior arrests.

African-American male clients. The men in the experimental group and in the comparison group were similar in terms of age, employment status, and level of education at the time of admission to the Drug Court program (see Table 2). Most participants in both groups were relatively young and had completed only 12 years or less of formal education. The average age of the men in both groups was 25. Fewer than half of the men in either group reported being employed.

	Table 1: Characteristics of Female Clients			
	Experimental (N = 24) %	(n)	Comparison (N = 26) %	(n)
Education at admission				
Less than 12 years	13%	(3)	27%	(7)
12 years	38%	(9)	31%	(8)
More than 12 years	33%	(8)	38%	(10)
Information not provided	17%	(4)	04%	(1)
Employment at admission				
Employed	63%	(15)	31%	(8)
Unemployed	29%	(7)	54%	(14)
Not in labor force	00%	(0)	12%	(3)
Information not provided	08%	(2)	04%	(1)
Reported Drug of Choice				
Marijuana/hashish	42%	(10)	35%	(9)
Cocaine/crack	75%	(18)	62%	(16)
Alcohol	50%	(12)	35%	(9)
Heroin	13%	(3)	15%	(4)

Proportions rounded to the nearest integer.

Table 2 also presents the drugs of choice reported by the men in the two groups. Polysubstance use was evident. Marijuana was a drug of choice by most men in both the experimental group (70%) and the comparison group (67%). Cocaine/crack and alcohol were also prominent as drugs of choice, with alcohol more prevalent in the experimental group.

Prior arrest information was not available for the men in the experimental group but data were available for 26 of the 30 men in the comparison group. The data indicated that 58% had been arrested once before, 30% had been arrested twice before, and 11% had no prior arrests.

RETENTION

The questions that pertained to "retention" in this study concerned whether the clients in the experimental group were more likely to remain substance-free and remain in treatment than their counterparts in the comparison group. A series of discriminant analyses were conducted to assess whether

Table 2: Characteristics of Afro-American Male Clients

	Experimental (N = 33) %	(n)	Comparison (N = 30) %	(n)
Education at admission				
Less than 12 years	33%	(11)	40%	(12)
12 years	48%	(16)	37%	(11)
More than 12 years	15%	(5)	13%	(4)
Information not provided	03%	(1)	10%	(3)
Employment at admission				
Employed	39%	(13)	40%	(12)
Self-employed	06%	(2)	00%	(0)
Unemployed	52%	(17)	50%	(15)
Information not provided	03%	(1)	10%	(3)
Reported drug of choice				
Marijuana/hashish	70%	(23)	67%	(20)
Cocaine/crack	36%	(12)	47%	(14)
Alcohol	55%	(18)	33%	(10)
Heroin	03%	(1)	00%	(0)

Proportions rounded to the nearest integer.

these two measures were significant indicators distinguishing between the experimental and comparison groups (see Table 3).

The analysis found that the retention level for female participants in the experimental group was significantly higher than that of the comparison group. Women in the experimental group remained in treatment significantly longer ($p < .001$) than their counterparts in the comparison group. The average length of time that comparison group members participated in the program was 5.5 months. In contrast, the women in the experimental group at the time of the research had been in the Drug Court program for an average of 13 months. A fairly strong positive within-group correlation was found for the number of months in the program (.694). The within-group correlation serves as a measure of the correlation between the values of the function that the discriminant analysis processes develop, and the values of each variable in the analysis.

The incidence of negative urinalysis test results was also found to be significantly higher ($p < .001$) for women in the experimental group than for women in the comparison group (see Table 3). A strong positive within-group correlation was found for the incidence of "clean" or negative urinalysis test results

Table 3: Discriminant Analysis of Indicators of Retention

Variable	Within-group correlation	F	Eigenvalue	Canonical correlation
Females*				
N months in program	.694	35.036**		
N negative urinalyses	.904	59.441**	1.547	.779
African-American Males*				
N months in program	.865	33.740**		
N negative urinalyses	.631	17.431**	0.717	.646

*Because data for one or more of the variables entered were missing, 4% of the female and 3% of the African-American male cases were excluded. **p < .001.

(.904). The women in the experimental group had negative urinalysis results only 33% of the time while experimental group members presented a negative urinalysis more than twice as often–85%.

As also indicated in Table 3, the African-American men in the experimental group remained in treatment significantly longer (p < .001) than the men in the comparison group. The average longevity of comparison group members was 7 months. In contrast, the experimental group members at the time of the study had been in treatment for an average of 15 months. The within-group correlation for months in the program (r = .8765) was strong.

The incidence of "clean" or negative urinalysis test results was also found to be significantly higher (p < .001) for African-American men in the experimental group than those in the comparison group. The within-group correlation for negative urinalysis (r = .631) is fairly strong. The African-American men in the comparison group had negative urinalysis results 50% of the time while those in the experimental group presented negative urinalysis results 92% of the time.

DISCUSSION

This study examined issues of race and gender in the treatment of offenders remanded to a Drug Court treatment program. A number of important findings emerged from this research relative to treatment programming.

The issue of retention is one that needs to be addressed by Drug Courts, particularly for substance abusers from groups that are at high risk of failure in treatment. "Therapeutic jurisprudence," the hallmark of Drug Courts, appears to be unable to consistently engage and rehabilitate the females and African-American males who utilize Drug Court treatment as an alternative to incarceration. Prior to the introduction of the specialized enhancement program, the legal inducement of court-monitored drug treatment had been insufficient to sustain the continued involvement of these client groups.

This research focused on females and African-American males who were identified by staff as being "non-compliant" with the expectations of Drug Court treatment. Nationally about 70% of Drug Court clients have been found to persist in treatment for a period of one year or more (Drug Court Clearinghouse, 1999). In this study, the average longevity of the "noncompliant" female and African-American male in what had been the "traditional" Drug Court treatment program was found to be only 5.5 and 7 months respectively. For the group of "noncompliant" clients in this study, participation in the "traditional" Drug Court treatment program was aborted long before one might reasonably have expected there to be positive treatment results (Peters and Murrin, 2000). In contrast, the average "noncompliant" female and African-American male in the specialized enhancement program persisted in treatment at least twice as long, and in most cases more than the hallmark of one year.

Findings in this study dispute assumptions that the presence of legal inducements to enter treatment, as reflected in the Drug Court procedures, can lead to successful treatment outcomes. The coercion prompting the criminal offender's enrollment in treatment is apparently insufficient to produce the level of engagement, motivation, and involvement needed for treatment retention and effectiveness. Treatment, in a sense, has been foisted upon the criminal offender and is likely perceived as being the lesser of two evils. The expectation that the option offered by Drug Courts and similar coercive programs of enrolling in treatment is sufficient to stimulate a reduction in substance abuse and related criminal behaviors appears to be simplistic. The involuntary client is highly resistant to treatment. Treatment success is painstaking to achieve. Initial treatment objectives are rudimentary and cautious, often seeking client cooperation and compliance rather than engagement and commitment. As a result, coercive treatment must focus on developing a level of motivation and commitment among clients that fosters retention. Thus, the challenge for any involuntary program is to maintain treatment involvement for a period of time sufficient to reduce the involuntary client's resistance and increase receptivity to treatment (Ritchie, 1986; Ivanoff, Blythe, & Tripodi, 1994).

This research returns to the classic question of "what works" in criminal justice interventions. In spite of the chorus of praise for Drug Court programs, our study offers cautious findings that the programs may have limited benefits for some criminal offenders. The Drug Court enhancement treatment program "tailored" to women and African-American males demonstrated its ability to achieve a level of retention greater than that of similar clients who had been in the less specialized "traditional" treatment program. This is particularly striking since the participants in the specialized program were women and African-American males who had been identified as being "at-risk" for failure in the "traditional" program.

The findings in this study of an enhanced Drug Court treatment program are suggestive. Contrary to the belief of some, particularly in the judicial community, the failure to graduate from the Drug Court program may not be a willful defiance of judicial authority (Tauber, 1994). Rather, what may be at work in a client's decision to drop out of the Drug Court program and face judicial sentencing for their crime is the failure of the design of the program. In this case study the specialized program sought to enhance the range and content of treatment services. The program tailored its interventions to the client group, incorporating a design reflective of a number of the strategies suggested in the treatment literature. The cultural experiences of the clients provided a schematic within which treatment was designed. Underpinning the treatment design was the premise that efforts to arrest substance abuse in consort with associated criminal behavior would be curtailed if close attention was not paid to the cultural experiences of offenders. The treatment design recognized that a monolithic approach was inappropriate. How clients define their experiences and problems is to a large extent rooted in their cultural experiences, attitudes, and perceptions. Their receptivity to treatment is also defined, in part, by the values, traditions, and expectations within which they have lived and grown. This is reflected, for example, in client attitudes towards authority figures, and towards the type of collectivity and self-expression that is fostered in group work (Carter and Helms, 1992). As Sue and Zane (1987) argue, the effectiveness of intervention strategies relies on the extent to which a client's problems and the approaches used for the resolution of those problems are compatible with the clients' cultural experiences and worldview.

This research investigated a small sample of clients in an innovative Drug Court treatment program in South Florida. The study found that the provision of specialized programming designed to address the differential needs of two types of clients was beneficial in its ability to increase the retention of clients in treatment. Self-examination and scrutiny are needed by Drug Court treatment programs about their effectiveness in serving the varied subgroups of their diverse client population. This research points to the importance of culturally specific programming, and of longitudinal research to monitor the short- and long-term impacts of such efforts. Within the past ten years, there has been a trend in numerous human service sectors to study their effectiveness and articulate what has been called "best practices." Since the Drug Court movement recently celebrated its tenth anniversary, such an initiative is long overdue.

REFERENCES

Amuleru-Marshal (1993). Political and economic implications of alcohol and other drugs in the African-American community. In L. Goddard (Ed.) CSAP Technical Report 6 (pp. 23-34). Rockville, MD: U.S. Department of Health and Human Services, pp. 23-34.

Atkinson, D. R., & Lowe, S. M. (1995). The role of ethnicity, cultural knowledge and conventional techniques in counseling and psychotherapy. In J. G. Ponterotto, J. M. Casas, L. A. Suzuki, and C. M. Alexander (Eds.), Handbook of multicultural counseling (pp. 387-414). Thousand Oaks, CA: Sage.

Belenko, S. (1998). Research on drug courts: A critical review. National Drug Court Institute Review, 1, and The National Center on Addiction and Substance Abuse, Columbia University. Available: http://www.drugcourt.org/docs/research.html.

Bell, P., & Evans, J. (1981). Counseling the black client: Alcohol use and abuse in Black America. City Center, MN: Hazelden Foundation.

Brisbane, F. (1992). Working with African Americans: The professional handbook. Chicago, Ill: HRDI International.

Carter, R. T. (1991). Cultural values: A review of the empirical research and implications for counseling. Journal of Counseling and Development, 70, 164-173.

Carter, R. T., & Helms, J. E. (1992). The counseling process as defined by relationship types: A test of Helm's interactional model. Journal of Multicultural Counseling and Development, 20, 181-201.

Drug Court Clearinghouse and Technical Assistance Project. (1999). Looking at a decade of Drug Courts. Washington, DC: American University. Available: http://www.american.edu/amerc.depts/spa/justice/decade1.htm.

Covington, S. S. (1998). Women in prison: Approaches in the treatment of our most invisible population. Women & Therapy, 21, 141-157.

DeLeon G., Melnick, G., Schoket, D., & Jainchill, N. (1993). Is the therapeutic community culturally relevant: Findings on race/ethnic differences in retention in treatment. Journal of Psychoactive Drugs, 25, 1, 77-86.

Duvall, H. J., Lock, B. Z., & Bill, L. (1963). Followup study of narcotic drug addicts five years after hospitalization. Public Health Rep, 78, 185-193.

Hodgins, D. C., El-Guebaly, N., & Addington, J. (1997). Treatment of substance abusers: Single or mixed gender programs. Addiction, 92, 7, 805-812.

Ivanoff, A., Blythe, B. J., & Tripodi, T. (1994). Involuntary clients in social work practice. A research-based approach. New York: Aldine De Gruyter.

Leukefeld, C. G., & Tims, G. M. (1990). Compulsory treatment for drug abuse. International Journal of the Addictions, 25, 6, 621-640.

Lewis, J. A. (1994). Issues of gender and culture in substance abuse treatment. In J. A. Lewis (Ed.), Addictions concepts and strategies for treatment (pp. 37-43). Gaithersburg MD: Aspen Publication.

Loneck, B., Garrett, J., & Banks, S. M. (1997). Engaging and retaining women in outpatient alcohol and other drug treatment: The effect of referral intensity. Health & Social Work, 22, 1, 38-46.

Maddux, J. F. (1988). The criminal justice client in drug abuse treatment. In C. G. Leukefeld, and F. M. Tims (Eds.), Compulsory treatment of drug abuse: Research and clinical practice (pp. 35-56). Rockville, MD: National Institute on Drug Abuse, 35-56.

McLellan, A. T., Hagan, T. A., Levine, M., Meyers, K., Gould, F., Bencivengo, M., Durrell, J., & Jaffe, J. (1999). Does clinical case management improve outpatient addiction treatment. Drug & Alcohol Dependence, 55, 1-2, 91-103.

Mejta, C. L. (1982). Sex related differences in the attribution of responsibility for heroin addiction: Implications for treatment. Dissertation Abstracts International, 42 (7-B), 2995.

Mejta, C. L., Bokos, P. H., & Mickenberg, J. (1997). Improving substance abuse treatment access and retention using a case management approach. Journal of Drug Issues, 27, 329-340.

Peters, R. H., & Murrin, M. R. (2000). Effectiveness of treatment-based drug courts in reducing criminal recidivism. Criminal Justice and Behavior, 27, 72-96.

Platt, J. J., Widman, M., Lidz, V., Rubenstein, D., & Thompson, R. (1998). The case for support services in substance abuse treatment. American Behavioral Scientist, 41, 8, 1050-1062.

Rapp, R. C., Siegal, H. A., Li, L., & Saha, P. (1998). Predicting postprimary treatment services and drug use outcome: A multivariate analysis. American Journal of Drug and Alcohol Abuse, 24, 603-617.

Ritchie, M. H. (1986) Counseling the involuntary client. Journal of Counseling and Development, 64, 516-518.

Schwartz, M., Baker, G., Mulvey, K. P., & Plough, A. (1997). Improving publicly funded substance abuse treatment: The value of case management. American Journal of Public Health, 87, 10, 1659-1664.

Simpson, D. D. (1988). National Treatment System Evaluation based upon the Drug Abuse Reporting Program (DARP) followup research. In F. M. Tims and J. L. Ludford (Eds.), Drug abuse treatment evaluation: Strategies, progress and prospects (pp. 29-41). Rockville, MD: National institute on Drug Abuse.

Sue, D. W., Arredondo, P., & McDavis, R. J. (1992). Multicultural counseling competencies and standards. A call to the profession. Journal of Counseling and Development, 70, 477-486.

Sue, S., & Zane, N. W. S. (1987). The role of culture and cultural techniques in psychotherapy: A critique and reformulation. American Psychologist, 42, 37-45.

Sullivan, W. P., Hartmann, D. J., & Dillon, D. (1994). Implementing case management in alcohol and drug treatment. Families in Society, 75, 67-73.

Sullivan, W. P., Wolk, J. L., & Hartmann, D. J. (1992). Case management in alcohol and drug treatment: Improving client outcomes. Families in Society, 73, 195-204.

Tauber, J. (1994) Treating Drug-using offenders through sanction, incentives. Corrections Today, 56, 1, 28-34.

Terrell, F. & Terrell, S. (1984). Race of counselor, client sex, cultural mistrust level, and premature termination from counseling among Black clients. Journal of Counseling Psychology, 31, 371-375.

Terry, W. C. (November 1993). Broward County Drug Court: A Preliminary Report. (Limited circulation.)

Terry, W. C. (1999). Broward County's dedicated drug treatment court: From post-adjudication to diversion. In W. C. Terry (Ed.) The early drug courts: Case studies in judicial innovations (pp. 77-107). Thousand Oaks, CA: Sage Publications.

Vontress, C. E. (1995). The breakdown of authority: Implications for counseling young African-American males. In J. G. Ponterotto, J. M. Casas, L. A. Suzuki, and C. M. Alexander (Eds.), *Handbook of multicultural counseling* (pp. 457-473). Thousand Oaks, CA: Sage Publications.

Wilenbring, J. L., Ridgely, M. S., Stinchfield, R., & Rose, R. (1991). Applications of case management in alcohol and drug dependence: Matching techniques and populations. Rockville, MD: National Institute on Alcohol Abuse and Alcoholism (ADM-911766).

AUTHORS' NOTES

Dr. Adela Beckerman is a program professor of Research and Evaluation at the Fischler Graduate School of Education and Human Services at Nova Southeastern University in Florida. She is also Associate Director of the Florida Inter-University Consortium of Child, Youth and Families Studies. Dr. Beckerman is a consultant with the Florida Education and Research Laboratory. Her previous publications have concerned welfare reform, child welfare, and corrections.

Dr. Leonard Fontana is a senior professor of Social and Behavioral Sciences at Broward Community College in Florida. He is also Director of the Florida Education and Research Laboratory. He is presently involved in a major study of a domestic violence and substance abuse treatment program in South Florida. His most recent published research was concerned with welfare reform in Florida.

Address correspondence to Dr. Adela Beckerman, Fischler Graduate School of Education & Human Services, Nova Southeastern University, 1750 NE 167th Street, North Miami Beach, FL 33162-3017.

Treatment "Dosage" Effects in Drug Court Programs

ROGER H. PETERS
University of South Florida

AMIE L. HAAS
University of South Florida

W. MICHAEL HUNT
University of South Florida

ABSTRACT This study assessed whether greater duration of involvement in a drug court program affected criminal justice outcomes. The major research hypothesis was that the length of participation in drug courts would be directly related to outcomes obtained during follow-up. Participants consisted of 226 individuals who entered two Florida drug court programs in Escambia and Okaloosa counties between June 1993 and June 1996. This sampling strategy was developed to insure that at least a one-year follow-up period was provided for each participant after discharge from the drug court program. Results indicate that the duration of time spent in a drug court program is significantly related to criminal justice outcomes, with greater time in the program associated with lower rates of follow-up arrest, and clearly support the importance of lengthy involvement in drug court programs and of expanded efforts to retain participants in these programs. *[Article copies available for a fee from The Haworth Document Delivery Service: 1-800-HAWORTH. E-mail address: <getinfo@haworthpressinc.com> Website: <http://www.HaworthPress.com> © 2001 by The Haworth Press, Inc. All rights reserved.]*

KEYWORDS Drug court, early treatment termination, recidivism, treatment dosage effects, treatment duration

In recent years, a large number of drug court programs have been developed throughout the U.S. that provide an alternative to incarceration for substance-involved offenders. Capitalizing upon criminal justice involvement as a window of opportunity to involve nonviolent substance abusing offenders in rehabilitation programs, drug courts facilitate cooperation and coordination among multiple community agencies in an effort to monitor and provide court-supervised treatment services. With the added goal of returning offenders to a socially productive way of life, most drug courts also require participants to seek and maintain employment, while helping them obtain vocational and other supplementary services (Peters & Murrin, 2000).

Previous research has established the efficacy of drug court treatment programs in reducing criminal recidivism for program graduates (Deschenes & Greenwood, 1995; Goldkamp, 1994; Tauber, 1994). However, research has not yet examined the effects of treatment "dosage" related to duration of program involvement on outcomes among program participants. Treatment dosage effects have been examined within the context of prison-based treatment programs, such as the "Stay'n Out" therapeutic community program in the New York State correctional system (Wexler, Falkin, & Lipton, 1990). In that study, successful parole outcomes (e.g., time until re-arrest and successful discharge from parole) for both males and females improved as time in the prison treatment program increased to 12 months, although outcomes began to decline after that point. Similar effects for duration of treatment have been observed in jail-based treatment programs (Swartz, Lurigio, & Slomka, 1996; Tunis, Austin, Morris, Hardyman, & Bolyard, 1996; Santiago, Beauford, Campt, & Kim, 1996). For example, arrest rates for offenders treated in a large residential jail program were inversely related to the duration of jail treatment, up to an optimal range of 91-150 days (Swartz, Lurigio, & Slomka, 1996).

To date, there has been little research available regarding treatment dosage effects in drug courts. The present study examined data from two drug court programs implemented in 1993 in Florida's First Judicial Circuit in Escambia and Okaloosa counties. Each of the programs provided at least one year of multi-modal substance abuse treatment, consisting of a wide range of services including comprehensive assessment, individual and group counseling, peer support groups, community support and aftercare groups, case management, and referral to ancillary services (e.g., mental health and vocational and educational services). Adherence to program guidelines was monitored through frequent and random drug testing, while judicial "status" hearings were used to monitor participants' abstinence and progress during the program (Peters & Murrin, 2000).

This study assessed whether greater duration of involvement in a drug court program affected criminal justice outcomes. The major research hypothesis was that the length of participation in drug courts would be directly related to outcomes obtained during follow-up. The study also examined demographic and substance use characteristics of participants to determine whether these variables affected retention in the drug court programs.

METHOD

Participants

Participants consisted of 226 individuals who entered two Florida drug court programs in Escambia and Okaloosa counties between June 1993 and June 1996. This sampling strategy was developed to insure that at least a one-year follow-up period was provided for each participant after discharge from the drug court program. This strategy also insured that the "lag" time (approximately six months) in entering local arrests to the National Crime Information Center (NCIC) and Florida Crime Information Center (FCIC) criminal justice databases would not affect the accuracy of outcome data obtained. The average participant was 31 years of age at time of entry into the program ($M = 31.11$, $SD = 7.49$ years), African-American (54.3% African-American, 45.7% Caucasian), and male (72.9% male, 22.1% female). Offenders in this sample had an average of over four arrests prior to entry into the drug court program ($M = 4.97$, $SD = 5.98$). Over half of the drug court participants in this sample (62.3%) entered the drug court intervention because of drug possession charges. Approximately half (49.5%) of the participants successfully completed the drug court programs.

Procedure

Information for the study was collected as part of a larger project examining treatment outcomes in the drug court programs. Data on the drug court participants were obtained from a number of archival sources including treatment records, probation records, records from the Clerk of the Court's office, and NCIC/FCIC records from the Pre-trial Release office. Following a review of existing records from these agencies, data coding protocols were developed to compile an outcome evaluation database. Evaluators consulted with staff from the above-mentioned agencies to design software and data entry procedures for computerization of evaluation data collected from each agency.

Treatment and court/criminal justice records were linked via unique identifying information, and were merged within a master data file that included descriptive information, longitudinal records of participants' drug court program involvement, and outcomes (e.g., re-arrest) during the follow-up period. Rigorous procedures were followed to protect the confidentiality of drug court participants involved in the study, with the staff carefully adhering to federal confidentiality laws and regulations governing the confidentiality of information obtained from research subjects (DHHS 42 C.F.R. Part 2). Evaluators worked with staff from the drug court programs and treatment agencies to modify existing informed consent procedures to address participation in the evaluation study.

Records regarding demographic and clinical information were obtained from treatment records and from drug court program and court records. Information regarding the participants' criminal history was obtained from NCIC and FCIC records gathered from the Escambia and Okaloosa County Pre-trial Release offices. Data coding protocols were developed to compile an outcome evaluation database for the drug court programs using the aforementioned sources. Evaluators consulted with staff from the respective agencies to design software and data entry procedures for computerization of evaluation data collected from each agency. Data were compiled from the various different databases and merged using unique identifying information (e.g., admission/discharge dates from the program and the Sheriff's Office ID/booking number) to protect confidentiality.

Measures

As described above, data were obtained through multiple sources. Clinical and demographic information was obtained from drug court treatment records. These treatment records included a comprehensive intake assessment and a substance abuse reporting form required by a state social service agency. The intake assessment included a range of demographic and background information as well as a description of other areas of psychosocial functioning, including mental health, medical, educational and vocational history, and admission diagnoses. Substance use patterns, treatment history, and evaluation of alcohol- and drug-related problems were measured using the Addiction Severity Index (ASI: McLellan et al., 1992). The ASI is a widely used standardized instrument that has been shown to provide reliable and valid information regarding psychological functioning related to drug and alcohol abuse, as well as psychological status, family and social functioning, medical status, and employment/financial support (McLellan et al., 1985).

Criminal history measures were obtained from NCIC/FCIC records. Criminal history information was manually coded from printed NCIC/FCIC records and provided information regarding arrest dates, primary charges, dispositions of charges, and sentences received. Probation records were also collected, which provided information regarding the demographic background history, education and employment, monthly wages and supplemental income, military history, current living arrangements, and arrests or violations reported in the last monthly reporting period. Records from the Clerk of the Court's Office provided data regarding the admission date to the drug court program, criminal charges leading to drug court admission, sentence status, length of supervision, dates of sanctions received and types of sanctions, dates of attendance at drug court status hearings, and date and type of discharge from the drug court program.

Because the database was composed of sources from multiple agencies, a systematic review of coded outcome evaluation data was completed to assess the reliability of the data collected, using a random sampling of 10% of participant records. This sampling included a review of each source of evaluation information examined in the study, including treatment, probation, and Clerk of the Court's office records. Results revealed an error rate of less than 1% for each type of record, suggesting that the information was accurately merged and coded.

RESULTS

As described in Table 1, drug court participants were assigned to one of five rationally derived groups, based on the number of days spent in the drug court program and program completion status. The first four groups covered 90-day intervals signifying the duration that non-graduates remained in the program (i.e., 0-90, 91-180, 181-270, and 271-365 days), while the fifth group included only drug court program graduates who remained in the program for at least 365 days. Criminal justice outcomes were evaluated at two time points: (1) 12 months following program admission, which was the anticipated duration of the drug court program, and (2) at 30 months after program admission. The data was analyzed using Analysis of Variance (ANOVA; alpha set at .05) with post hoc Fisher's Least Squares Difference (LSD) tests conducted to evaluate group differences. Finally, contingency tables were created to analyze differences between early and late terminators from the program with regard to demographic and descriptive variables.

Table 1: Characteristics of "Treatment Dosage" Groups

Days Spent in Program/ Completion Status	N	% of sample
Non-Graduates (n = 114)		
0 - 90 days/non-graduate	36	15.9%
91 - 180 days/non-graduate	22	9.7%
181 - 270 days/non-graduate	25	11.1%
> 270 days/non-graduate	31	13.7%
Graduates		
Graduate (≥ 365 days)	112	49.5%

Consistent with prior studies, individuals who successfully completed the program had significantly lower rates of arrest during follow-up than drug court participants who did not graduate. However, even among non-graduates, the duration of time spent in the drug court program was significantly related to rates of follow-up arrest at the 12-month follow-up period, $F(4, 221) = 21.87, p < .01$. As shown in Table 2, arrest rates were lowest for individuals who graduated from the program. In fact, arrest rates were significantly lower for graduates compared to all non-graduate groups, even when considering non-graduates who remained in the program for more than nine months (Fisher's LSD = $-.65, p < .01$). Similarly, follow-up arrest rates generally declined in relation to the amount of time spent in the drug court program. For example, individuals who were terminated from the program after at least nine months of participation had significantly lower rates of arrest during the 12-month follow-up period than individuals who were terminated from the program during the first three months of participation (Fisher's LSD = $-1.05, p < .01$), and in comparison to individuals who were terminated after three to six months in the program (Fisher's LSD = $-.63, p < .05$), or after six to nine months in the program (Fisher's LSD = $-.65, p < .05$).

Comparable results were found when examining arrest rates during the full 30-month follow-up, $F(4, 221) = 16.65, p < .01$. As with the results found at the 12-month follow-up time point, program graduates had significantly lower rates of arrest, even when compared to non-graduates who remained in the drug court program for at least nine months (Fisher's LSD = $-1.12, p < .01$). As shown in Table 2, arrest rates at the 30-month follow-up were highest for individuals who left the program in the first three months, with rates of re-arrest generally declining as a function of the duration of time spent in the drug

Table 2: Follow-Up Arrests by "Treatment Dosage" Group

	M	SD	Range	% Arrested
12-Month Follow-Up				
Non-graduates with 0-90 days in program	1.92	1.78	0-8	72.2%
Non-graduates with 91-180 days in program	1.50	1.60	0-6	68.2%
Non-graduates with 181-270 days in program	1.52	1.08	0-4	84.0%
Non-graduates with > 270 days in program	0.87	1.20	0-6	54.8%
Graduate ($\geq$ 365 days)	0.22	0.53	0-3	17.9%
30-Month Follow-Up				
Non-graduates with 0-90 days in program	3.11	2.63	0-13	80.6%
Non-graduates with 91-180 days in program	2.68	2.51	0-8	81.8%
Non-graduates with 181-270 days in program	2.12	1.36	0-5	88.0%
Non-graduates with > 271 days in program	1.84	2.00	0-9	74.2%
Graduate ($\geq$ 365 days)	0.71	1.12	0-5	42.0%

court program. Only 18% of drug court graduates were arrested during the 12-month follow-up period and 42% were arrested during the 30-month follow-up, in comparison to substantially higher proportions for each of the non-graduate groups.

A second purpose of the present study was to investigate whether demographic or descriptive variables could be used to predict early termination (e.g., within the first three months) from the drug court program, in comparison to participants who remained in the program for a longer time but who did not graduate. Analyses using a series of ANOVA's with post hoc LSD tests revealed no significant differences for the variables examined, including gender, ethnicity, participant's drug of choice, number of different substances used by the participant, number of prior arrests, educational level, prior history of abuse (physical, sexual, or emotional), marital status, education, and motivation for treatment at time of entry into the program.

DISCUSSION

This study examined treatment dosage effects in two community-based drug court programs in Florida. Results indicate that the duration of time spent in a drug court program is significantly related to criminal justice outcomes, with greater time in the program associated with lower rates of follow-up arrest. For both the 12- and 30-month follow-up periods, there was a striking linear relationship between the duration of time in drug court programs and the rate of arrest. While drug court graduates fared better than each of the non-graduate groups during the follow-up periods, outcomes also tended to improve for non-graduates as the amount of time in treatment increased. These findings are consistent with those obtained from studies examining jail and prison treatment outcomes. A second goal of this study was to identify characteristics of drug court participants that predict who will be successfully retained in the program over time. Numerous demographic and descriptive variables were examined, but none distinguished early program dropouts from late program dropouts.

Findings indicate that while graduation from drug court programs is desirable, there also appear to be dose-related treatment benefits that accrue for non-graduates as well. Results clearly support the importance of lengthy involvement in drug court programs and of expanded efforts to retain participants in these programs. Efforts to enhance retention are particularly needed for youthful offenders, female participants with a history of polydrug use and prostitution, and participants with co-occurring mental health disorders. Drug court programs also need to expand efforts to address the specialized needs of cultural minorities (e.g., through peer mentoring and vocational training and placements) in order to retain participants over time. Newly refined technologies such as contingency contracting and motivational interviewing should be implemented within drug courts to examine their impact on program retention.

Additional work is clearly needed to identify factors contributing to early dropout from drug court programs. Several program features (e.g., the personality and level of involvement of the judge, attorneys, probation officer, and drug court treatment liaison) that are unique to drug courts may affect drug court program retention and have not yet been explored in other community treatment settings. Although demographic and other descriptive variables did not effectively distinguish between early and late program dropouts in this study, other client-related factors merit further investigation, such as the level of community and family support, and employment status. Drug court policies related to sanctions and incentives should also be explored to determine their impact on retention.

Treatment dosage effects identified in this study signal the need for additional research examining follow-up outcomes among participants who have successfully completed drug court programs of varying duration (e.g., 6 months, 12 months). For example, random assignment of drug court participants to programs of varying duration would allow for comparison of cost-effectiveness of these programs and would potentially allow for development of profiles of drug court participants who could be "matched" effectively to these different programs. Further research is also needed to calibrate the effects of treatment dosage on other salient drug court outcomes, such as substance abuse, employment, and utilization of health care services.

REFERENCES

Deschenes, E. & Greenwood, P. (1995). Drug court or probation? An experimental evaluation of Maricopa County's drug court. *The Justice System Journal 18*, 55-73.

Goldkamp, J.S. (1994). Miami's treatment drug court for felony defendants: Some implications for assessment findings. *Prison Journal, 73*, 110-166.

McLellan, A.T., Kushner, H., Metzger, D., Peters, R.H., Smith, I., Grissom, G., Pettinati, H., & Argeriou, M. (1992). The fifth edition of the Addiction Severity Index. *Journal of Substance Abuse Treatment, 9*, 199-213.

McLellan, A.T., Luborsky, L., Cacciola, J., Griffith, J., Evans, F., Barr, H.L., & O'Brien, C.P. (1985). New data from the Addiction Severity Index: Reliability and validity in three centers. *Journal of Nervous and Mental Disease, 173*, 412-423.

Peters, R.H., & Murrin, M.R. (2000). Effectiveness of treatment-based drug courts in reducing criminal recidivism. *Criminal Justice and Behavior, 27*(1), 72-96.

Santiago, L., Beauford, J., Campt, D., & Kim, S. (1996). *SISTER Project Final Evaluation Report: Sisters in Sober Treatment Empowered in Recovery, San Francisco County Sheriff's Office Department*. The Clearinghouse for Drug Exposed Children, University of California, San Francisco.

Swartz, J.A., Lurigio, A.J., & Slomka, S.A. (1996). The impact of IMPACT: An assessment of the effectiveness of a jail-based treatment program. *Crime and Delinquency, 42*, 553-573.

Tauber, J.S. (1994). Drug courts: Treating drug-using offenders through sanctions, incentives. *Corrections Today*, 28-30, 32-33, 76-77.

Tunis, S., Austin, J., Morris, M., Hardyman, P., & Bolyard, M. (1996). *Evaluation of drug treatment in local corrections*. Washington, DC: National Institute of Justice.

Wexler, H.K., Falkin, G.P., & Lipton, D.S. (1990). Outcome evaluation of a prison therapeutic community for substance abuse treatment. *Criminal Justice and Behavior, 17*(1), 71-92.

AUTHORS' NOTES

Roger H. Peters, PhD, is a professor in the Department of Mental Health Law and Policy at the Louis de la Parte Florida Mental Health Institute (FMHI), University of South Florida, where he has been a faculty member since 1986. Dr. Peters also serves as the Coordinator of the FMHI Collaborative for Substance Abuse Treatment and Policy Research, and is an adjunct professor with the Department of Rehabilitation and Mental Health Counseling. He received his PhD in clinical psychology from the Florida State University, following completion of a pre-doctoral internship at the University of North Carolina. Dr. Peters has pursued research, consultation, and training initiatives involving substance abuse treatment within the criminal justice system. He has published frequently in major journals, served on federal expert panels, grant and document reviews, national advisory boards and committees, and has served as a consultant to AJA, CSAT, CMHS, NIC, NIJ, NIDA, OJP, and other federal and state agencies. Dr. Peters has recently served on the Board of Directors of the National Association of Drug Court Professionals.

Amie L. Haas earned her PhD from the University of South Florida in clinical psychology in 2001 and is presently a postdoctoral fellow at the Substance Abuse Treatment Research Center at the University of California, San Francisco, where she is involved in studies examining pharmacological interventions for smoking cessation. She has been involved in several other projects examining drug courts, including program evaluation of the Florida First Judicial Circuit Drug Courts and examining gender differences in the trajectory of substance abuse problems among drug court offenders.

W. Michael Hunt earned the BS at James Madison University and the Master of Arts degree from Hollins University, both in Virginia. He is a member of the staff at the Louis de la Parte Florida Mental Health Institute studying substance use issues in offenders and other special populations and a doctoral candidate in clinical psychology at the University of South Florida.

Address correspondence to Dr. Roger H. Peters, Louis de la Parte Florida Mental Health Institute, Department of Mental Health Law and Policy, 13301 N. Bruce B. Downs Boulevard, Tampa, FL 33612-3807 (E-mail: peters@fmhi.usf.edu).

Drug Courts in Operation: Current Research. Pp. 73-85.
© 2001 by The Haworth Press, Inc. All rights reserved.

Employment Issues Among Drug Court Participants

MICHELE STATON

University of Kentucky Center on Drug and Alcohol Research

ALLISON MATEYOKE

University of Kentucky Center on Drug and Alcohol Research

CARL LEUKEFELD

University of Kentucky Center on Drug and Alcohol Research

JENNIFER COLE

University of Kentucky Center on Drug and Alcohol Research

HOLLY HOPPER

University of Kentucky Center on Drug and Alcohol Research

TK LOGAN

University of Kentucky Center on Drug and Alcohol Research

LISA MINTON

Kentucky Administrative Office of the Courts

ABSTRACT The overall goal of the current study, which was funded by the National Institute on Drug Abuse (Grant #DA13076), was to develop and evaluate an enhanced Drug Court employment intervention with the goals of improving drug treatment retention and reducing recidivism. Focus groups were conducted with Drug Court clients in order to gain a better understanding of employment needs in order to target and refine the enhanced employment intervention. As expected, findings indicate that Drug Court participants encounter a variety of employment issues. Perhaps the major theme that emerged is the consistent difficulty expressed by participants in balancing work and treatment involvement. Implications from this study provide important insights for developing employment interventions, as well as for further research. *[Article copies available for a fee from The Haworth Document Delivery Service: 1-800-HAWORTH. E-mail address: <getinfo@haworthpressinc.com> Website: <http://www.HaworthPress.com> © 2001 by The Haworth Press, Inc. All rights reserved.]*

KEYWORDS Drug court, focus group methods, employment needs, employment readiness, social skills training

Efforts in the criminal justice system over the past decade have focused on developing and implementing treatment alternatives to incarceration for substance abusing offenders, of which one approach is the Drug Treatment Court. Drug Courts provide court mandated, comprehensive interventions designed to control criminal activity and drug use among offenders who are living in the community (CASA, 1998). Over 100,000 drug offenders have participated in Drug Court programs nationwide since their inception in 1989 (American University, 1998), and nearly 71% of participants have successfully completed Drug Court or remain involved in Drug Court (US General Accounting Office, 1997).

The benefits of Drug Courts have been described as: (a) reduced recidivism; (b) decreased drug use while participants are in the program; (c) increased birth rates of drug-free babies to once-addicted mothers; (d) increased access to alumni and mentoring groups; (e) increased efforts by clients at long-term relapse prevention efforts; and (f) cost-effective treatment (Belenko, 1998; OJP, 1997). An additional benefit for Drug Court participants is the opportunity to obtain and retain employment since almost all Drug Court programs provide vocational training and job development (OJP, 1997). This is considered a benefit as employment services may be needed and wanted by drug abusers, but extensive employment assistance is not generally part of drug treatment (Platt, 1995; Schottenfeld et al., 1992).

Positive treatment outcomes have also been related to pretreatment employment (Wickizer et al., 1994). Recent studies have shown that regular employment enhances self-esteem, provides a stable source of income, and offers an environment removed from a substance-using subculture (Belenko & Peugh, 1998). Stable employment has also been related to decreases in substance use and criminal activity (Bachman et al., 1997; Kandel and Yamagichi, 1987; Sampson & Laub, 1993).

Since poorly paid, entry level service employment is widely available in the US (Burtless, 1997), these entry-level jobs become the usual sources of employment for Drug Court participants. Nevertheless, unrealistic expectations often occur when drug-abusing clients expect higher paying positions and higher salaries, but do not possess employment skills comparable to their employment expectations (French et al., 1992; Berk, Leinihan, & Rossi, 1980). Uggen (1999) reported that high-quality jobs decreased the likelihood of criminal behavior independent of criminal history and substance use. Consequently, while attaining employment is important for many ex-offenders, job retention and upgrading to a higher quality job are also important.

The project described herein builds upon completed process evaluation pilot work with Kentucky Drug Court participants. These pilot evaluations revealed that only 23% of clients were working full-time before entering Drug Court, and those with stable employment demonstrated greater drug treatment retention and successful treatment outcomes (CDAR, 1998; Logan, Leukefeld, & Williams, 1999). In light of these findings, the Drug Court judges expressed interest in enhanced Drug Court employment activities. Kentucky Drug Court judges indicated that getting a job is a minimal requirement for participants, which provides a foundation for gaining job skills, maintaining successful employment, and achieving promotions to upgrade their employment. Thus the purpose of the overall project is to build upon the existing services provided by Drug Courts and to focus interventions on obtaining, maintaining, and upgrading employment for Drug Court clients.

Over the duration of the on going project, a sample of Drug Court participants from two Kentucky Drug Courts will be recruited and randomly assigned to an employment focused intervention group or to a control group (Drug Court as usual). Those in the intervention group will receive the enhanced employment intervention, which is designed to coincide with the three phases of Drug Court treatment. Treatment includes outpatient groups, AA/NA groups, and individual sessions focusing on addiction as well as criminal thinking and takes the average client 18 months to complete (see Table 1).

For clients randomly assigned to the enhanced employment intervention group, treatment will be complemented by job skill training, social skill training (Leukefeld et al., 2000), strengths based case management (Siegal et al., 1996), and motivational interviewing (Prochaska & DiClemente, 1986). Pre- and posttest data will be collected from the intervention as well as the comparison group at baseline, graduation/termination, six months, and 12 months after Drug Court graduation/termination.

Phase	Approximate Time	Tasks
		☐ **Table 1: Drug Court Phases**
One	1 month	• attend one Drug Court session per week • provide all assigned drug screens each week • attend and document 12-step support meetings • attend all assigned groups, family and/or individual counseling sessions • begin to make payments toward Court obligations • maintain Court-approved stable housing • maintain Court-approved employment training and/or educational referrals • turn in journal assignments • comply with any necessary medical referrals • purchase a NA or AA text book • begin work on a 12-step recovery program • obtain a sponsor
Two	8 - 10 months	• attend one Drug Court session every other week • begin payment of restitution and court costs • complete assigned readings • maintain daily physical activity • do at least one good deed per court appearance
Three	4 months	• similar responsibilities as phase 2 • attend one Drug Court session every three weeks, • pay a substantial amount of restitution • regularly mentor a new Drug Court participant and/or group session • complete an exit calendar, exit interview, and plan for aftercare

The employment intervention is grounded in established job readiness and life skill training modules that are designed for individuals involved in the criminal justice system. Focus groups were conducted with Drug Court clients in order to gain a better understanding of employment needs in order to target and refine the enhanced employment intervention. Specifically, focus groups were used to: (a) examine how Drug Court participants obtained previous employment, (b) discuss issues which supported keeping and maintaining a job, and (c) identify specific skills needed to upgrade employment. Findings from these focus groups are presented in this paper.

METHOD

Participants

A purposive sample of 56 (20 female and 36 male) Drug Court clients participated in five separate focus groups. Participants were selected from three

Kentucky Drug Courts. Demographic information was not collected from focus groups' clients. However, a recent process evaluation indicated that Kentucky Drug Court participants are similar to national Drug Court clients (American University, 1998; CDAR, 1998) with an average age of 32 and 12 years of education. In addition, two-thirds were African American, and over half (61%) reported they had never been married. Nearly one-fourth (23%) reported chronic health problems, almost one in five reported emotional abuse, 15% reported physical abuse, and 7% reported any sexual abuse. Self-reported mental health symptoms were high with forty percent self-reporting depression, 47% reporting anxiety, 19% reporting suicidal thoughts in the month preceding the interview, and one in four reporting using medication for psychological problems. Family involvement with substances was high with 40% reporting at least one family member with a drug or alcohol problem and almost two-thirds (62%) reported having at least one family member with psychological problems.

Procedure

Focus groups were used to identify employment needs and issues Drug Court clients face. Generally, focus groups are used to collect qualitative data from group interaction to produce insights and information (Morgan, 1988). These focus groups allowed for more in-depth, and sometimes sensitive, conversations about obtaining, maintaining, and upgrading employment. Table 1 contains a brief description of each Drug Court treatment phase. Completing each phase and promotion to the next phase is determined by the individual's performance, completion of the assigned tasks, and cooperative behavior.

Focus group participants were selected from Phase Three of the Drug Court program since Phase Three participants were not eligible for project recruitment. Each focus group lasted about one hour, and participants were paid $15. The focus groups were conducted in a group room at each of the three Drug Court offices. A moderator guided group discussion, while a co-moderator recorded responses. Focus group questions were grounded in the literature and included:

1. What kinds of things do you wish you'd known when you were looking for a job?
2. How did you get your last job?
3. Was getting a job different after you entered Drug Court?
4. What helped you keep your longest job?
5. How is keeping a job different for a person in Drug Court?
6. What do you need to do to get a better job?
7. What are the things that can be done to help Drug Court participants get better jobs?

The following introduction was used for each focus group:

> Thank you for taking time to meet with us today. My name is (*moderator*). You have been asked to participate in this focus group because you are currently involved in Drug Court. We are developing an employment program for Drug Courts, and we are interested in your opinions about employment. For this group, I will be asking questions to help our discussion. Everything we say today is strictly confidential. The project has a Federal Certificate of Confidentiality and has been approved by the University of Kentucky human subjects committee to protect your confidentiality. (*Co-moderator*) will be recording things said, but your name will not be used in any way. We are interested in hearing what you have to say. We are here to learn from you. There are no right or wrong answers, and we ask that everyone's opinion be respected. It is important that we hear from everyone. We're very interested in your opinions and views. We ask that only one person talk at a time. You will be paid $15 for your participation; please be sure to fill out the payment form before you leave. Does anybody have any questions about the study or this focus group?

Focus Group Themes

Qualitative content methods were used to develop themes by analyzing narrative data obtained through the focus group interviews (Miles & Huberman, 1994; Staton et al., 2000). Respondents' comments followed three major themes, which paralleled the protocol questions. However, as expected, a number of other issues emerged. The primary themes are discussed below.

Obtaining a Job

At Drug Court entry, participants agree to adhere to the Drug Court schedule including regular court appearances, weekly groups, AA/NA meetings, and random urine drug screening. Focus group participants indicated that the Drug Court schedule often conflicts with 9:00 to 5:00 work schedules, thereby making it necessary to obtain a job that provides flexible hours or night shifts. In addition, a Drug Court requirement is to obtain stable employment. Consequently, seasonal jobs or part-time jobs with irregular hours are not permissible. Participants indicated that they often settle for jobs that are not satisfying in order to meet the Drug Court employment requirements, which is reflected in a participant's statement, "You may just take a job that you don't like, just to have a job."

Another issue among participants related to obtaining a job included job-seeking skills. For example, when participants were asked how they located their last job, several mentioned reading the newspaper, temporary employment services, and friends or family contacts. Others mentioned local career resource centers, assistance from Drug Court staff, going door to door, and sheltered workshops. One participant commented, "There are lots of jobs out there; if you can't find one, you're just not looking." Other participants indicated that they would like to know more about employers who were likely to hire Drug Court participants, and that establishing a network of services with these employers would facilitate job searches. Along the same lines, participants wanted to know which employers do not conduct background checks so their records would not prohibit them from getting a job. Interest was also expressed about appropriate ways to present references on job applications, which included who to list, who not to list, how to contact references in advance, and formatting references. Job interviews were also of interest to clients as well. Specifically, participants were interested in learning what to wear, how to sit, appropriate answers to "tough" interviewing questions, and how to deal with being asked about their "past." Focus group participants also mentioned a desire for help in preparing resumes, particularly since many participants have limited work experience or large gaps of time between jobs that are "difficult to explain." Thus, it was apparent that job skill training should constitute an important part of the employment intervention.

In addition to a demanding Drug Court treatment regimen, participants identified several barriers to obtaining employment. For example, most participants indicated that the major barrier to obtaining employment was having a felony conviction. One male noted that, "It's always in the back of an employer's mind–the fact that you're a felon. They should give you a probation period in order to give you a chance." Participants indicated that once a potential employer learned about their criminal record, potential employers no longer considered them. One participant said, "The police record just kills you." Other barriers to obtaining employment included inadequate education and work experience. Some participants had difficulties using public transportation to a job, particularly in rural areas. Others, particularly women, indicated that limited or no childcare was a barrier to finding and keeping a job.

Maintaining a Job

The overwhelming majority of focus group participants indicated that the main reason for keeping a job was the need for stable income. Several participants were single parents who depended upon their salaries and benefits to provide for their children. Some considered themselves fortunate to have a job that paid a good salary, which was a motivating factor for maintaining employment. Another important reason for maintaining employment was a positive work environment including co-workers and a respectful employer. In fact, one participant indicated, "It's really nice when they [employer] recognize how important you are and the work you do." Participants recognized the advantage of an employer who understands the Drug Court schedule and makes allowances for demands. Finding a job with flexible hours and an understanding employer affects the ability of Drug Court participants to maintain employment during their treatment. Several participants indicated that they were able to maintain employment because they enjoyed their job and found work challenging. One woman indicated, "I love to work with people. My job as a cashier makes that possible, and it also gives me a lot of responsibility with the money. I like to be trusted." Other participants mentioned they enjoyed being busy and recognized that having structure in their schedule decreased idle time.

As with obtaining employment, keeping a job is also different in Drug Court. Employment is often monitored by employer contacts and with receipt payment documentation by Drug Court staff. If Drug Court participants leave a job, they must have another job prearranged and approved by their Drug Court counselor. If clients are unable to find a job immediately, or if they leave a job without approval, they can temporarily meet their employment requirement with community service. However, given the pressures associated with working a stable job and meeting program requirements, focus group participants reported feeling stress in balancing their personal lives and families. "There is a lot to keep straight in my life–Drug Court, making it to work, making it to groups, and having to find sitters"; "Having to make classes, meetings, drops and keep a job is really hard and takes a lot of planning and discipline"; "I usually make sacrifices in my personal life–I just can't get it all done." Consequently, adapting to a treatment schedule and a new lifestyle also impacts maintaining employment.

Upgrading a Job

A common finding across focus groups was that participants indicated that the key to getting a better job was having an education, experience, and training. Having a high school diploma or a GED is required before graduating from Drug Court. However, most participants said they needed additional vocational training or college in order to upgrade their employment. "Most high-paying places won't even talk to you unless you've got at least some college." Therefore, help with taking college entrance exams, obtaining college financial aid information, and getting information on vocational training programs were identified as needs.

Participants also expressed a need for more information about careers and job openings. "It's important to know where to find good jobs, and where you can find jobs that have opportunities to advance and make more money." Participants expressed interest in using a job developer with community job networks, particularly those who hire ex-offenders. Differences across Drug Court sites related to job development activities and community employer networks. Several Drug Court participants indicated that they had "a good sense of employers" who would hire ex-offenders while others had no idea. Several clients emphasized the importance of an understanding supervisor–which they indicated could be more difficult to find in "the better jobs." For example, "It would be nice if employers could be educated about addiction. Just because we've made some mistakes, we're not necessarily bad employees. Just because I had a drug problem doesn't mean I can't do a good job." "It's hard to hire a recovering addict if you don't understand addiction."

The need for job readiness skills which included interviewing, filling out employment applications, writing cover letters, and developing resumes was also identified. In fact, several participants indicated that they had resumes, but didn't feel comfortable using them to get a "better" job. "I would love to be able to update my resume with my new job experiences, I would like for it to look good." In addition, several participants expressed interest in completing a skills assessment and specifically wanted to know the types of jobs that would be suitable matches for their skills. Finding a job that a participant wanted was underscored as being important for upgrading employment.

A final theme that emerged was that upgrading employment seems to depend on accessing better jobs. For example, women seemed more likely to settle for either a childcare job or a job that enabled them to work flexible hours in order to meet their own childcare obligations. Consequently, for women, getting a "better job" was tied to financial opportunities as well as to benefits including childcare and insurance. It was also noted that in rural areas, access to jobs was affected by transportation. In fact, both rural males and females indicated they could not rely on public transportation, which is a major barrier to seeking certain jobs. While public transportation was available in urban areas, it can be unreliable and time-consuming.

CONCLUDING REMARKS

As expected, focus group findings indicate that Drug Court participants encounter a variety of employment issues. Perhaps the major theme that emerged is the consistent difficulty expressed by participants in balancing work and their drug court involvement. This finding is consistent with other studies which reported that drug abusers can have limited job related skills, particularly time management skills, the ability to meet role expectations, and difficulty in setting priorities (Kinney & Leaton, 1995). The Drug Court schedule is restrictive in comparison to the participants' lifestyles when they used drugs. Managing life commitments during this phase requires good time management, particularly with the imposed structure and work demands that can and frequently do collide with Drug Court schedules and family needs. Given these demands, the employment intervention should include time management skills so participants can improve chances for their success.

Focus group participants indicated they often settled for less than satisfactory jobs in order to meet Drug Court employment requirements. Consequently, attitudes toward work range from impartial to negative. A somewhat surprising finding was the inconsistency of responses received about attitudes toward work. Some participants indicated they were "into their jobs" and Drug Court requirements suited their needs. Other participants seemed apathetic and almost removed from the process, while others were dissatisfied and bitter about "having" to work. Perhaps this is related to this phase of Drug Court treatment–or perhaps it is related to their stage of recovery. It is also possible that there is an unknown factor related to job satisfaction for some who do not have extensive employment histories or skills, but are court mandated to work. Targeting the intervention and tailoring it for each participant is part of the challenge.

Another consistent theme that emerged from focus group discussions was that most participants wanted help in job readiness training and searching for a job. This finding is supported in the literature that identifies distinct employment needs for drug users (Platt, 1995). While many offender-based programs provide some type of pre-release planning or job readiness training, it is uncertain how these programs increase job opportunities and reduce drug use, recidivism, relapse, and crime. Focus group participants were interested in obtaining employment skills that included: interview preparation, resume writing, and job application skills, as well as skills to upgrade to a better job. Participants also indicated that a major employment issue is finding employers who were likely to hire ex-offenders. Consequently, Drug Court participants indicated that they would benefit from a network of services with employers who would hire Drug Court participants. In fact, studies show that, while the general attitude of employers is hesitant about hiring ex-offenders, these relationships can be enhanced with incentives such as tax breaks, bonding, networks, and finding skilled, qualified, and dependable employees (Albright & Denq, 1996).

Based on these focus groups, specific information can be incorporated into employment interventions. For example, focus group participants indicated they were struggling with balancing work, Drug Court involvement, and family responsibilities. With this in mind, group sessions can be designed to target these areas, as well as time management. Networking and job development were also mentioned. Assisted job development could be incorporated which can be followed by self-directed job development to upgrade employment. Job readiness training including resume writing, job interviewing, and completing applications could be incorporated. Focus group participants indicated that emphasis should be placed on answering questions related to previous convictions and discussion on how these questions could be answered. Participants also indicated that increased educational and training opportunities should be made available which include scholarships, financial aid, grants, and other support. Sessions should cover issues related to overcoming job related barriers such as childcare and transportation—which are particularly important for women and rural residents.

There are limitations to this study. Participants were a small purposive sample of Drug Court clients in Kentucky. For this reason, results may not be generalizable to other Drug Court clients or other substance-abusing offenders. In addition, there is a potential bias of responses given the focus group setting, despite assured confidentiality. Regardless of these limitations, implications from this study provide important insights for developing employment interventions, as well as for further research. While the issues affecting employment need to be further explored, these focus group findings suggest that Drug Court participants are expected to obtain a job and maintain stable employment. While employment can be considered extremely important to their recovery, Drug Court participants often encounter job retention issues related to their criminality and addiction. Research should continue to examine these issues in order to better understand employment service needs for substance abusing offenders.

REFERENCES

Albright, S. & Denq, F. (1996). Employer attitudes toward hiring ex-offenders. *The Prison Journal*, 76, 118-137.

American University. (1998). *Looking at decade of Drug Courts*. Washington, DC: U.S. Department of Justice Drug Court Clearinghouse and Technical Assistance Project.

Bachman, J.G., Wadsworth, K.N., O'Malley, P.M., Johnson, L.D., & Schulenbarg, J.E. (1997). *Smoking, drinking, and drug use in young adulthood*. Mahwah, NJ: Earlbaum.

Belenko, S., & Peugh, J. (1998, Fall). Fighting crime by treating substance abuse. *Issues in Science and Technology*, Fall, 53-60.

Belenko, S. (1998). Research on Drug Courts: A critical review. *National Drug Court Institute Review, I(1)*, pp. 1-30.

Berk, R.A., Leinihan, K.J., & Rossi, P.H. (1980). Crime and poverty: Some experimental evidence from ex-offenders. *American Sociological Review, 45*, 766-86.

Burtless, G.T. (1997). Welfare recipients' job skills and employment prospects. *The Future of Children: Welfare to Work, 7(1)*, 39-51.

CASA–Center on Addiction and Substance Abuse. (January 1998). *Behind bars: Substance abuse and America's prison population.* New York: Columbia University.

Center on Drug and Alcohol Research. (1998). *Drug Court process evaluation.* Lexington, KY: University of Kentucky, Center on Drug and Alcohol Research.

French, M.T., Dennis, M.L, McDougal, G.L., Karuntzos, G.T., & Hubbard, R.L. (1992). Training and employment programs in methadone treatment: Client needs and desires. *Journal of Substance Abuse Treatment, 9*, 293-304.

Kandel, D.B. & Yamaguchi, K. (1987). Job mobility and drug use: An event history analysis. *American Journal of Sociology, 92*, 836-878.

Kinney, J. & Leaton, G. (1995). *Loosening the grip: A handbook of alcohol information.* St. Louis, MO: Mosby-Year Book.

Leukefeld, C., Godlaski, T., Clark, J., Brown, C. & Hays, L. (2000). *Behavioral therapy for rural substance abusers.* Lexington, KY: University Press of Kentucky.

Logan, TK, Leukefeld, C., & Williams, K. (1999). *Drug Court program process evaluation.* Lexington, KY: University of Kentucky, Center on Drug and Alcohol Research.

Miles, M.B., & Huberman, A.M. (1994). *Qualitative data analysis.* Thousand Oaks, CA: Sage.

Morgan, D.L. (1988). *Focus Groups as Qualitative Research.* Newbury Park, CA: Sage.

OJP. (January, 1997). *Defining Drug Courts: The key components.* U.S. Department of Justice Programs. Drug Court Programs Office.

Platt, J.J. (1995). Vocational rehabilitation of drug abusers. *Psychological Bulletin, 117*, 416-433.

Prochaska, J.O., & DiClemente, C.C. (1986). Toward a comprehensive model of change. In W. Miller and N. Heather (Eds.), *Treating addiction behaviors*, pp. 3-27. New York: Plenum.

Sampson, R.J. & Laub, J. (1993). *Crime in the making.* Cambridge, MA: Harvard University Press.

Schottenfeld, R.S., Pascale, R., & Sokolowski, S. (1992). Matching devices to needs: Vocational services for substance abusers. *Journal of Substance Abuse Treatment, 9(1)*, 3-8.

Siegal, H.A., Rapp, R.C., Kelliher, C.W., Wagner, J.H., O'Brien, W.F., & Cole, P.A. (1996). The role of case management in retaining clients in substance abuse treatment: An exploratory analysis. *Journal of Drug Issues, 27*, 821-831.

Staton, M., Leukefeld, C., & Logan, TK. (In press). Health service utilization and victimization among incarcerated female substance abusers. *Substance Use and Misuse.*

Uggen, C. (1999). Ex-offenders and the conformist alternative: a job quality model of work and crime. *Social Problems, 46*, 127-151.

US General Accounting Office. (1997). *Drug courts: Overview of growth, characteristics, and results.* GAO/GGD-97-106. Washington, DC: USGAO, July.

Wickizer, T., Maynard, C., Atherly, A., Frederick, M., Koepsell, T., Krupski, A., & Stark, K. (1994). Completion of clients discharged from drug and alcohol treatment programs in Washington State. *American Journal of Public Health, 84*, 215-221.

Wolkstein, E. & Spiller, H. (1998). Providing vocational services to clients in substance abuse rehabilitation. *Directions in Rehabilitation Counseling, 9*, 65-78.

AUTHORS' NOTES

Michele Staton, MSW, CSW, is a research coordinator at the University of Kentucky, Center on Drug and Alcohol Research. She is the study director for two National Institute of Health (NIH) funded projects, one examining the health service utilization of incarcerated substance abusers, and the other enhancing Drug Court retention through an employment intervention.

Allison Mateyoke, BA, is a data coordinator for the Drug Court Employment project by recruiting and interviewing subjects for the project and developing intervention modules for the employment intervention. Prior to this project, she worked as data collector and coordinator for the Health Services Utilization project.

Carl Leukefeld, DSW, is a professor of Psychiatry and Behavioral Science at the University of Kentucky, and the Director of the Center on Drug and Alcohol Research. He has given numerous presentations and written articles focused on treatment, criminal justice, prevention, and AIDS.

Jennifer Cole, BS, is a data coordinator at the University of Kentucky, Center on Drug and Alcohol Research. She is the study director for a NIDA funded study, examining the nature, extent, and co-occurrence of HIV risk behavior, victimization, and drug use among crack users.

Holly Hopper, MRC, is an employment specialist for the University of Kentucky Center on Drug and Alcohol Research Drug Court Enhancement Project. She is responsible for the implementation and clinical aspects of the employment intervention with Drug Court clients.

TK Logan has a PhD in applied psychology and is currently an assistant professor at the University of Kentucky, Center on Drug and Alcohol Research. Dr. Logan has been funded by the National Institute on Drug Abuse (NIDA) to examine the nature, extent, and co-occurrence of HIV risk behavior, victimization, and drug use among crack users.

Lisa Minton was appointed manager of the Drug Courts division of the Administrative Office of the Courts (AOC) when the division was established July 1, 1996. Prior to that, she was a field supervisor for Pretrial Services, an AOC statewide program. She has also managed an adult literacy program and taught GED classes in rural Kentucky. She oversees Kentucky's 10 operational adult and 5 operational juvenile sites; 21 pilot/planned adult and 11 pilot/planned juvenile sites; and one planned family drug court site. The Fayette and Jefferson Drug Courts are National Mentor training sites. Ms. Minton has been a speaker at a wide array of state and national training sessions and has co-authored several publications on Kentucky's drug courts.

The research reported here was supported by the National Institute on Drug Abuse, Grant DA13076. The opinions expressed here are those of the authors and not the funding agency or the University of Kentucky.

Address correspondence to Michele Staton, MSW; Center on Drug and Alcohol Research, 643 Maxwelton Court, Lexington, KY 40506 (E-mail: cmstat00@pop.uky.edu).

Predictors of Engagement in Court-Mandated Treatment: Findings at the Brooklyn Treatment Court, 1996-2000

MICHAEL REMPEL

Center for Court Innovation

CHRISTINE DEPIES DESTEFANO

Urban Institute, Justice Policy Center

ABSTRACT Past research indicates that more time in treatment yields better post-treatment outcomes, with 90 days of treatment often identified as a minimum threshold for achieving positive results, thus making it important to identify factors that predict meaningful engagement in treatment and to devise policies to assist subgroups facing a high risk of dropping out. Although a literature currently exists on voluntary treatment programs, fewer studies examine dynamics specific to court-mandated programs such as drug courts. Those programs use legal coercion applied via the threat of incarceration, coupled with ongoing court supervision, to motivate participants to succeed. Results were analyzed at the Brooklyn Treatment Court. Analyses looked at retention for at least 90 days of treatment, and engagement, defined as completing four consecutive months of drug-free and sanction-less participation. Multivariate analyses revealed that the level of *legal coercion*, measured by expected incarceration time in the event of program failure, strongly predicted both retention and engagement. Also predictive was the legal/emotional coercion faced by participants who indicated at intake that they had a pending Family Court case whose outcome might hinge on the drug court outcome. Participation during the 30-day period immediately following program entry was as important as coercion. Warranting or failing to begin treatment within 30 days of formal entry strongly predicted dropping out. The following additional characteristics predicted dropping out: younger, primary drug of heroin, prior misdemeanor conviction(s), and residence in a neighborhood characterized by greater *social isolation*. Policy implications of all findings are discussed. *[Article copies available for a fee from The Haworth Document Delivery Service: 1-800-HAWORTH. E-mail address: <getinfo@haworthpressinc.com> Website: <http://www.HaworthPress.com> © 2001 by The Haworth Press, Inc. All rights reserved.]*

KEYWORDS Drug court, ethnicity, legal coercion, race, recidivism, social isolation, socioeconomic status, substance abuse history, treatment duration, treatment engagement

The substance abuse treatment literature consistently links more time in treatment to more favorable outcomes on measures such as drug use, criminal activity, and employment (Anglin et al., 1989; Collins and Allison, 1983; DeLeon, 1988(a); DeLeon, 1988(b); Hubbard et al., 1989; Lawental et al., 1996; Peters and Murrin, 1998; Siddall and Conway, 1988; Taxman, 1998; Taxman et al., 1999; Trone and Young, 1996). Some studies identify 90 days of treatment as a minimum threshold for achieving positive outcomes (e.g., De Leon 1984; Hubbard et al., 1989; Simpson, 1979, 1981; Simpson, Joe, and Brown, 1997). Yet, fewer than half of the participants in most community-based programs are retained for 90 days (De Leon and Schwartz, 1984; Joe and Simpson, 1976). Understanding why many participants abandon treatment prematurely, while others become seriously engaged, presents a critical challenge for the treatment community.

It was originally believed that participants voluntarily seeking treatment were more motivated and more likely to succeed in treatment than coerced participants. However, evidence is now mounting that coerced treatment is as effective as voluntary treatment at producing favorable outcomes (Anglin et al., 1989; Belenko, 1999; Collins and Allison, 1983; DeLeon, 1988(a); DeLeon, 1988(b); Hubbard et al., 1989; Lawental et al., 1996; Siddall and Conway, 1988; Trone and Young, 1996). Some programs, such as the Brooklyn Drug Treatment Alternative-to-Prison (DTAP), report a higher retention rate among their defendant population than non-defendants referred to comparable community-based treatment programs (Trone and Young, 1996). Responding to this evidence, court-mandated treatment programs proliferated during the 1990s, and national anti-drug policies broadened from interdiction and enforcement to put more emphasis on treatment. Court-mandated programs are characterized by the application of legal coercion, usually via the threat of incarceration, to motivate participants to succeed. Programs using the *drug court model* generally differ from earlier court-mandated programs by incorporating more intensive court supervision. Most drug courts require participants to report regularly for evaluation by a court-employed case manager and the drug court judge. Responding to progress, the judge uses a system of intermediate rewards or sanctions, including temporary jail stays, in an effort to motivate participants to remain in treatment.

With the recent explosion of drug courts, it is important for research to identify key characteristics associated with treatment retention among a court-mandated population and to develop effective policies to assist those facing a high risk of dropout. Yet, current studies analyzing predictors of success primarily focus on a voluntary population (Hiller, Knight, and Simpson, 1999), and few studies examine programs using the drug court model (for exceptions, see Peters, Haas, and Murrin, 1999; and Schiff and Terry, 1997). Although several locally funded drug court evaluations show predictors of retention, their methodologies are unknown, and their results were not disseminated except as project reports provided to the funder. For a summary of results from these evaluations, see Belenko (1998, 1999). The existing gap in the literature is addressed here by analyzing predictors of treatment engagement at the Brooklyn Treatment Court (BTC), a program for substance-abusing persons arrested in Brooklyn, New York.

THE SIGNIFICANCE OF LEGAL COERCION

Legal coercion has repeatedly been found critical in motivating participants to begin treatment and, once there, to remain in treatment (Anglin et al., 1989; Collins and Allison, 1983; DeLeon, 1988(a); DeLeon, 1988(b); Hubbard et al., 1989; Lawental et al., 1996; Peters and Murrin, 1998; Siddall and Conway, 1988; Trone and Young, 1996). For example, Trone and Young (1996) examined repeat felony defendants (facing three to six years in prison) participating in the Drug Treatment Alternative-to-Prison (DTAP) program and found that 63% were still in treatment at one year. In drug courts nationwide, Belenko (1998) estimates that 60% of participants were in treatment at one year. By comparison, only half of the participants in outpatient drug-free programs nationwide were still in treatment after just three months (Simpson et al., 1997). Trone and

Young attributed the high DTAP retention rate to the "credible threat of incarceration to keep people in treatment until their improvement begins to motivate them to finish the program" (1996: 9). Nonetheless, other studies found no relationship between legal status and treatment retention (Joe and Simpson, 1976; Sansone, 1980; and Simpson and Friend, 1988). Hiller et al. suggest that these "inconsistencies might be due in part to the variety of indicators used as estimates of legal pressure" (1998: 466).

Our review revealed primarily two analytic strategies for measuring legal coercion, and each has methodological limitations. One popular strategy is to study participants enrolled in community-based programs, distinguishing between those who are and are not subject to outside legal supervision (Anglin et al., 1989; Hiller et al., 1998). For example, Hiller and colleagues classified participants as facing low, medium, and high legal pressure and find that those under moderate and high pressure were more likely to be retained at 90 days than were those under low pressure. However, the low pressure group did not have *any* formal legal status, thus making it difficult to establish whether the moderate and high pressure groups were more likely to be retained due to legal coercion per se or due to other aspects of their legal involvement (e.g., court supervision, encouragement by parole or probation officers, regular drug-tests, etc.).

A second analytic strategy is to focus on participant *perceptions* as to the level of coercion facing them. For example, Young, Dynia, and Belenko (1996) found, using a sample consisting only of court-involved participants, that those *perceiving* greater legal pressure were likely to remain in treatment longer, even though objective program features did not vary systematically across participants. While clearly informative, this strategy leaves untested the impact of more *objective* differences in the level of coercion facing different participants: e.g., whether participants factually facing more incarceration time do better. Testing this is important, since it is easier for programs to manipulate their objective features than to affect the psychological processes underlying each participant's perceptions. Accordingly, we developed a measure classifying the objective level of coercion facing different Brooklyn Treatment Court participants.

OTHER PREDICTORS OF TREATMENT ENGAGEMENT

Much research has studied other factors affecting treatment success outside a court-mandated population. This section reviews those factors found generally relevant. Some of the contradictory findings reported below underscore the difficulty in distinguishing which factors predict treatment success and failure. In some instances, better theorization is needed to explain *why* certain relationships hold, as opposed to merely reporting results and then relating them to past results (which sometimes differ).

Personal Characteristics

Previous findings suggest that persons who are young, female, less educated, unemployed, and dependent on a highly addictive drug are at higher risk of treatment dropout.

Age. Research consistently shows that throughout the United States and other industrialized societies, criminal behavior peaks in late adolescence and gradually declines thereafter (e.g., Hirschi and Gottfredson, 1983; Farrington, 1986). Most explanations note that adolescents and young adults are particularly likely to seek autonomy and status through involvement in deviant peer groups, whereas deviant peer involvement diminishes as persons age (Hirschi and Gottfredson, 1983; Moffitt, 1993). Correspondingly, it is plausible that older persons tend to be more receptive to rehabilitative policy interventions such as drug courts. Another explanation for the "aging out" phenomenon among a substance-abusing population may be that over time, persons grow tired of their addicted lifestyle. Saxon reasons, "it makes sense that as opioid addicts grow older, increasing dissatisfaction with their addict life-styles, health concerns, and other factors associated with aging may make them more amenable to treatment" (1996: 1206). Indeed, several studies report that older participants are retained in treatment longer than younger participants (Grella et al., 1997; Mammo and Weinbaum, 1991; Sansone, 1980; Saxon, 1996).

Sex. In general, treatment outcomes for women are poorer than for men (Beckman, 1979; Mammo and Weinbaum, 1993; Wilsnack, 1982). In their analysis of 12,697 alcoholics admitted to outpatient treatment centers, Mammo and Weinbaum (1993) found that 48.8% of the women dropped out of treatment whereas 38% of the men dropped out. However, Mammo and Weinbaum cautioned that educational background may be a confounding variable, since the women in their study were more likely to lack college training (1993: 96). Poorer outcomes may also result because women are more often the primary caretakers of young children and sick family members, possibly creating external barriers to their ability to attend treatment. The literature suggests a need to control more carefully for confounding variables in pinpointing if and why sex-based differences exist. (See Beckerman & Fontana, this volume.)

Race/Ethnicity. To date, studies assessing race and treatment outcome have produced different results. Some conclude that race is significant (Peters and Murrin, 1998; Steer, 1980; Sansone, 1980; Saxon et al., 1996), while others report no relationship (Condelli and Hubbard, 1994; McFarlain et al., 1977).

Mammo and Weinbaum (1991) found that it is more likely for white and "other" race/ethnic groups than blacks and Hispanics to complete treatment. However, when social, demographic, and economic variables were controlled, they found that race is no longer significant. As with the analysis of sex, this highlights the need to control for socioeconomic variables. Additionally, it is important for research to study treatment programs designed specifically for different ethnic groups, since nonwhites may be particularly prone to drop out when treatment programs are not culturally sensitive to their needs (Beauvais, 1998; Fisher et al., 1996; Westermeyer, 1995).

Socioeconomic Status. Research indicates that higher socioeconomic status predicts better outcomes. Several studies report a positive relationship between educational background and treatment success (Hiller et al., 1998; Mammo and Weinbaum, 1991; Sampson et al., 1978). Other studies report a positive relationship between employment and treatment success (Hiller et al., 1999; Hser et al., 1990-91; Mammo and Weinbaum, 1991; McLellan et al., 1983(a); Siddall and Conway, 1988; Steer, 1980). One explanation may be that those higher in socioeconomic status have more to lose economically by continuing to abuse drugs. A second explanation derives from the social control theory of deviant behavior (Hirschi, 1969; Kornhauser, 1978; Sampson and Laub, 1993) which proposes that crime and other forms of social deviance become more likely when ties to mainstream social institutions are attenuated. Alternatively, when persons are significantly invested in mainstream social ties, for instance by becoming involved in a stable marriage, educational pursuits, or employment, they are more likely to avoid criminal behavior or to desist from prior criminal behavior (see also Laub, Nagin and Sampson, 1998).

Substance Abuse History. The literature indicates that the more addictive the participant's primary drug of choice (e.g., heroin, cocaine, crack) the more difficult it is to break the addiction (Grella et al., 1997; O'Donnell et al., 1976; Robins, 1980; Peters and Murrin, 1998; Peters, Haas, and Murrin, 1999; Young, Dynia, and Belenko, 1996). The severity of the addiction, as measured by the amount, duration, and frequency of chemical use (McLellan et al., 1980, 1982), is also associated with post-treatment outcomes (Babor et al., 1988; Stanton, 1980). The literature on *prior treatment episodes* has produced differing results. On one end of the spectrum, some researchers found that failed prior treatment episodes predict attrition in future episodes (Beckman and Bardsley, 1986; Brown et al., 1982/1983; Leigh et al., 1984; Siguel and Spillane, 1978). On the other end, Maglione et al. (2000) found that those who reported prior treatment experiences were less likely to drop out. Still others reported no relation (Ball et al., 1988; Feigelman, 1987; Steer, 1983a, 1983b; Steer and Kotzker, 1978; Szapocznik and Ladner, 1977). Stark pointed out that the "effects of prior treatment history are confounded with age and longevity and severity of drug use" (1992: 103). Young participants with no prior episodes may drop out at a higher rate because of their age whereas older patients with extensive prior treatment may be retained due to their maturity.

Criminal History. Criminological research consistently demonstrates that prior delinquency is associated with future delinquency (Elliott and Menard, 1996; Thornberry et al., 1994). Elliott and Menard (1996) explained that interaction with *delinquent peers* tends to precede the onset of delinquency and to independently predict future delinquency (see also Elliott et al., 1985; Jensen, 1972; Matsueda and Heimer, 1987). Corresponding with this research, some studies of voluntary treatment participants report that those with more prior arrests are disproportionately likely to drop out (Babst, 1971). Similarly, in a study of coerced participants, Young, Dynia, and Belenko (1996) found that those with more prior *prison* sentences (which involve at least one year of incarceration) were retained for less time on average.

Other Personal Characteristics. Two additional variables have been found predictive of treatment retention, although they were not included in the present study. First, participants with little or no *family/emotional support* tend to have poorer treatment outcomes (Connor, 1998; Kingree, 1995; McLellan et al., 1992; Siddall and Conway, 1988). In this paper, the available measure of family support was whether the participant lived with family members at intake; but this measure was deemed inappropriate, since family members may themselves be addicts or a loving/supportive relationship may be absent. Following social control theory referenced earlier, we expected that emotional/family support would show a positive impact on retention only if family members were themselves integrated into the mainstream social structure. Since we believed we did not have an appropriate measure for family/emotional support that would take into account these issues, we did not include this variable. Second, psychiatric history has been an important variable in other studies, with the literature showing poorer retention rates and outcomes among a dually diagnosed population (Gottheil et al., 1992; McLellan et al., 1981, 1983(a), 1983(b); Rounsaville et al., 1987; Zuckerman et al., 1975). BTC does not use an effective, validated screening instrument to diagnose mental health disorders other than substance abuse. Hence we could not test the impact of mental health status.

Neighborhood Social Isolation

Previous research links neighborhood social isolation to a higher propensity for crime, drug use, single-parent households, and other social dislocations (e.g., Anderson, 1990; Jargowsky and Bane, 1991; Wilson, 1987, 1997). *Social isolation* applies to neighborhoods with widespread poverty, weak social institutions (e.g., schools, churches, or industry), and few gainfully employed adult role models. Wilson (1987) argues that in neighborhoods high in social isolation, residents confront fewer social controls that might deter criminal behavior, substance abuse, and other forms of social deviance. Accordingly, neighborhoods high in social isolation may not provide a supportive environment for substance abuse recovery. Yet, a review of the literature resulted in no studies testing the impact of neighborhood social isolation on treatment outcomes.

Participation Immediately After Program Entry

Few studies assess the relationship between developments in the period immediately after a participant agrees to enter treatment and subsequent outcomes. One study by Leigh et al. (1984) examined treatment outcomes among 172 alcoholic patients attending an outpatient program. They found that a delay of more than 14 days from assessment to first appointment was a key discriminating variable between those who failed to show for treatment at all versus those who kept at least one appointment. However, that study did not report the eventual treatment completion rate for those who did show for at least one appointment. So it is possible that the majority of those participants dropped out of treatment prematurely as well. Other studies analyzing waiting time and treatment retention reveal conflicting results. Joe (1994) found that limiting the waiting time for placement into a substance abuse program did not affect attrition, while Maddux (1993) found that a two-week delay in admission resulted in a loss of 25% of substance abusers seeking treatment. And Mundell (1994) reported that addicts placed on waiting lists returned to their addict lifestyle and lost their motivation for change by the time a treatment slot became available.

Summary/Hypotheses

Previous research illuminates the overall effectiveness of coerced treatment for a defendant population (e.g., see especially reviews in Belenko, 1998, 1999). Not yet established are the critical factors that *predict* treatment outcomes, leading some court-mandated participants to begin with a better or worse chance of success than others. Extrapolating from the above body of research that mainly did *not* focus on a court-mandated population, the following may be hypothesized.

H1. Coercion: *Increased legal coercion is related to probability of treatment engagement.*

H2. Personal Characteristics:
    2a. *Probability of treatment engagement varies positively with age.*
    2b. *Women are more likely to drop out of treatment than men.*
    2c. *Probability of treatment engagement varies positively with socioeconomic status.*
    2d. *Number of mainstream social ties (e.g., to family, work, or school) is related to probability of treatment engagement.*
    2e. *Addiction severity is positively related to a probability of treatment dropout.*
    2f. *Prior criminal behavior is positively related to probability of treatment dropout.*
H3. Neighborhood Social Isolation: *Living in a neighborhood higher in social isolation is related to probability of treatment dropout.*
H4. Early Program Participation: *Following program entry, rapid initiation into treatment is related to probability of subsequent engagement.*

BROOKLYN TREATMENT COURT OPERATIONS

Data for analysis came from the Brooklyn Treatment Court (BTC), which serves substance-abusing persons arrested on felony drug charges in Brooklyn, New York. Since opening in June 1996, BTC has operated as a demonstration project implemented under the stewardship of the Center for Court Innovation, a nonprofit court development organization. Until September 2000, BTC was only open to defendants arrested in three of five geographic zones of Brooklyn and is now institutionalized as a permanent part of the Brooklyn court system.

BTC participation begins after a potential participant pleads guilty to an eligible drug charge and agrees to a *treatment mandate*, which stems from the charges in the plea agreement and the participant's criminal history. Participants also agree up front to a jail or prison alternative that will be imposed in the event of program failure. The four BTC treatment mandates are:

1. *Misdemeanor:* Participants pleading guilty to a misdemeanor are mandated to a minimum of 8 months in BTC and typically face 6 months in jail if they fail the program. (Although all BTC participants are arrested on felony drug charges, some reach plea agreements enabling them to plead guilty to a misdemeanor.)
2. *First Felony:* Participants pleading guilty to a first felony are mandated to a minimum of 12 months in BTC and typically face 1 year in either jail or prison if they fail the program.

3. *Multiple Felony:* Participants pleading guilty simultaneously to two or more felonies are mandated to a minimum of 18 months in BTC and typically face a minimum prison sentence of 1 1/2 years if they fail the program.
4. *Predicate Felony:* Participants pleading guilty to a *predicate* felony (i.e., pleading guilty to a felony and having at least 1 prior felony conviction) are mandated to a minimum of 18 months in BTC and typically face a minimum prison sentence of 3 years. Thus the minimum time in BTC is the same for multiple and predicate felons, but predicates face more prison time if they fail.

The four treatment mandates are divided into three *phases of treatment.* To complete Phase One, participants must complete *four consecutive months of drug-free and sanction-less participation.* The four months must be consecutive. Therefore, if a participant goes out on a warrant or tests positive for drugs before four months, the count starts over again. This makes it more challenging to complete Phase One than simply to total four cumulative months of treatment time. Since relapses and other program violations are common in each Phase–and especially at the beginning of Phase One–most *successful* participants spend more time in BTC than their minimum mandate requires. For example, of those completing Phase One, the median completion time is 8.2 months, over twice the four-month minimum. To complete Phase Two and Phase Three, participants must total additional predetermined numbers of consecutive drug-free and sanction-less months. (The minimums for participants with the misdemeanor mandate are 2 months in Phase Two and 2 months in Phase Three. The minimums for participants with the first felony mandate are 4 months in Phase Two and 4 months in Phase Three. And the minimums for participants with either the multiple or predicate felony mandates are 6 months in Phase Two and 8 months in Phase Three.)

As in most drug courts, BTC employs intensive court supervision requiring regular court appearances (usually once per month) for a drug test, case manager visit, and appearance before the BTC judge. Responding to participant compliance, the judge administers a system of graduated rewards and sanctions. To reward progress, the judge can offer verbal encouragement, requests for courtroom applause, or formal certificates of achievement. To sanction relapses or other infractions, the judge can require extra court visits, reassign participants to a more intensive treatment regimen, order temporary jail stays, or choose from a long list of other sanctions, depending on what seems appropriate. The judge can also fail participants for repeated non-compliance and incurring of sanctions, a violent or otherwise ineligible new arrest (e.g., due to heavy drug trafficking), or because the participant voluntarily opted-out and requested the incarceration alternative.

DATA AND METHODOLOGY

The Sample

Analysis is based on participant status at the end of June 2000 for the 1163 participants who entered BTC at least one year earlier. The one-year time frame was chosen to allow sufficient time to elapse for participants in the study to definitively complete or not complete Phase One. Nonetheless, 6% (70) of the sample had an indeterminate completion status and were excluded from most analyses.

Measures

Treatment Retention. Treatment retention is a dichotomous variable measuring whether the participant completed 90 days of treatment. When measuring 90 days of treatment, *indeterminate* status was applied to participants who had not yet completed 90 days but were still actively pursuing treatment, meaning that at the time of the analysis, their status was *in compliance* and under program supervision. We reasoned that these participants may eventually complete 90 days and therefore should not be grouped with the dropouts. Indeterminate status participants were not included in the analysis. A second subset of participants who had not yet officially failed the program but had been out on a warrant for more than 30 days as of the analysis were defined as dropouts.

Treatment Engagement. Treatment engagement is a dichotomous variable measuring whether the participant completed Phase One. Indeterminate status was applied here to two subgroups. The first consisted of those who had not yet completed Phase One but were still actively pursuing treatment (see explanation above). The second consisted of those who had not yet completed Phase One and had been out on a warrant for more than 30 days as of the analysis but had previously completed 90 days of treatment. We reasoned that these participants had previously made sufficient progress to render plausible a scenario in which they return from their warrant and complete Phase One. A separate analysis indicated that this scenario is approximately as plausible as not. Of those who entered BTC at least two years ago, completed 90 days of treatment, but were out on a warrant as of the one-year point, 38% eventually returned from their warrant and completed Phase One, 42% eventually dropped out, and 20% still lacked final completion status after two years. Since either completion outcome is possible, it was deemed inappropriate to place participants out on warrant after 90 days of treatment but before completing Phase One in either the completed or dropped-out categories. However, test analyses (results not shown) were conducted for multivariate models reported on in Table 2, in which warranted participants *were* redefined as dropouts. All findings in these test models were substantively identical to those in Table 2, except that many of the p-values rose slightly. This was interpreted as a logical outcome of including participants as dropouts whose status should really be indeterminate.

Coercion. BTC has built-in differences in the objective level of legal coercion facing different participants because each of the four BTC treatment mandates corresponds with a progressively longer incarceration alternative. Such objective variations in coercion are unusual in court-mandated programs studied to date. For the analysis, we constructed a 4-category scale for whether the participant faced the misdemeanor, first felony, multiple felony, or predicate felony treatment mandate.

The BTC data capture a second form of coercion by measuring whether participants indicated at intake that they had a pending Family Court case to gain or retain custody of one or more of their children. Given project staff knowledge of participants, a "yes" response on the Family Court item was interpreted to indicate that a pending Family Court case exists and that this case was meaningful to the participant. "No" or "don't know" responses were not interpreted to indicate the lack of Family Court cases, as some participants may be involved in such a case but may not respond affirmatively due to a lack of attachment.

Personal Characteristics. At an intake interview generally occurring the next business day after arraignment, potential BTC participants are administered a comprehensive psychosocial assessment. Responses to this assessment were used to establish key personal characteristics. Basic demographics included in the analysis were sex, age, race/ethnicity, and educational background. Race/ethnicity was recoded into 3 categories: Hispanic/Latino (both white and nonwhite), black, and Caucasian or other. Due to a lack of variance in the education measure, education was recoded into a dichotomous variable for whether the participant graduated high school. Additionally, two variables were included concerning the participant's *mainstream work and social ties*. A dichotomous variable was constructed for whether the participant was either employed or in school at intake. Although past research has not joined employment and educational status in this way, theoretically, we considered that *either* employment or school participation should signify daily interaction with mainstream social controls (hypothesis 2d). Second, a variable was included to measure whether the participant was ever homeless. From prior analyses with the BTC data, it was found that a *history of homelessness* is more revealing than *current* homelessness. Participants with a history of homelessness may have weak social support networks from families or friends and may consequently be subject to weak social controls. Also, for some, a history of homelessness may be tied to mental illness, but we could not test this, since the BTC assessment does not use a validated screening instrument for mental health disorders.

Regarding substance abuse history, *primary drug of choice* is a categorical variable based on self-report of the primary drug of choice: heroin, crack, marijuana, and other (subsuming non-crack cocaine, alcohol, and a small number of other responses). *Prior treatment episodes* is a measure based on the participant's self-report of previous substance abuse treatment (0, 1, 2, or 3 or more previous episodes). Also, a *drug addiction severity index* measuring the duration, frequency, and method of substance abuse was included in test regressions but eventually excluded, due to statistical insignificance and possible multi-colinearity stemming from its strong inter-correlation with primary drug.

Nearly all *criminal history* data was provided by the New York State Division of Criminal Justice Services (DCJS). Criminal history variables used in the analysis were whether the participant had at least one prior misdemeanor conviction and whether the participant had at least one prior felony conviction.

Neighborhood Social Isolation

Neighborhood social isolation was operationalized with two variables based on the participant's *zip code* (used as the best available proxy for neighborhood). First, we constructed a *social isolation* score based on the product of (a) the percent of households with an annual income under $15,000, (b) the females-to-males ratio, and (c) the percent of residents younger than 18 years old. The latter two measures tap the percent of single-parent, female-headed households. Wilson (1987) identified a high prevalence of these households to indicate social isolation. Second, we included a variable for the percentage of black residents to test whether discrimination may have led to neighborhood-based disadvantages in predominantly black neighborhoods. Although our primary theoretical interest was in whether there was an impact of historical discrimination faced by African-Americans, in a test model, we included a variable for the percentage of minority residents (either black or Latino). This variable was insignificant in all bivariate and multivariate analyses. All zip code-based measures were constructed from demographic data compiled by Caci Marketing Systems (1999) and drawing on 1990 census data, official census projections for changes between 1991 and 1996, and Caci projections extending to 1999. Homeless participants were assigned the median statistic for all zip code-based variables.

Participation Immediately After Program Entry

Two variables were intended to assess progress within the 30 days immediately following a guilty plea and agreement to enter BTC. The first was a dichotomous variable measuring whether the participant disappeared from program contact, prompting issuance of a police warrant, within the initial 30-day post-entry period. The second was a dichotomous variable measuring whether the participant attended at least one day of treatment within 30 days of entry. These variables were affected by a third, *days to first treatment placement*, which is the number of post-entry days it takes the BTC case manager to locate a suitable community-based treatment provider. Median days to first placement were 10 (17 for women and 7 for men). Multivariate analyses excluded days to first treatment placement due to its exceptionally strong inter-correlation with attending at least one day of treatment within 30 days ($r = .535$, $p < .001$).

RESULTS

Rates of Treatment Engagement

Figure 1 presents *completion rates* for 90 days of treatment and Phase One. For 90 days of treatment, 70% completed, 30% dropped out, and less than 1% had indeterminate status. For Phase One, 58% completed, 36% dropped out, and 6% had indeterminate status. Thus approximately 10% fewer participants completed Phase One than 90 days of treatment, confirming our expectation that Phase One is a more challenging marker of treatment engagement than the strictly quantitative 90 days measure.

Bivariate Analyses

Table 1 presents descriptive and correlational statistics for the predictor variables. Concerning descriptive information on BTC participants, some of the more salient statistics include the following:

- Thirty-eight percent of the participants were female and 62% were male.
- Thirty-eight percent of participants were Hispanic/Latino, 54% black, and 7% Caucasian or other.
- Participants face more severe socioeconomic disadvantages than the general population. Only 18% of participants were employed or in school at intake, and 28% were currently or formerly homeless. Furthermore, only 39% of BTC participants completed high school, 11% had any college education, and 2% completed four years of college. (The last two percentages are not displayed in Table 1.)
- Heroin (36%) and crack (36%) were the most prevalent primary drugs of choice, followed by marijuana (14%), alcohol (6%), non-crack cocaine

(6%), and all others (2%). Twenty-seven percent report one prior treatment episode, 10% report two prior episodes, and 12% report three or more.
- Thirty-five percent of participants had at least one prior misdemeanor conviction and 20% had at least one prior felony conviction.
- Thirty-three percent pled to the misdemeanor treatment mandate, 53% to the first felony, 5% to the multiple felony, and 9% to the predicate felony mandate.
- Seven percent of participants (14% of females and 3% of males) said they had a pending Family Court case.

As hypothesized, the bivariate correlations (last two columns of Table 1) indicate that coercion *increases* the probability of treatment engagement. Receiving a more serious treatment mandate and having a pending Family Court case both correlated with Phase One completion. Regarding personal characteristics, older, black, and participants naming crack as their primary drug of choice were more likely to complete Phase One, whereas Latinos and participants naming heroin were more likely to drop out. Also, participants with at

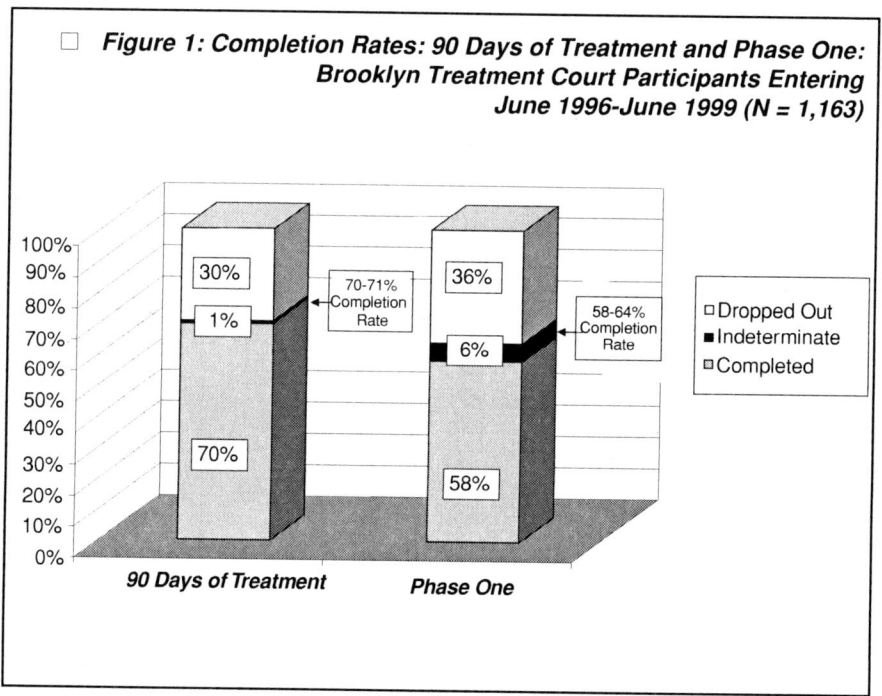

Figure 1: Completion Rates: 90 Days of Treatment and Phase One: Brooklyn Treatment Court Participants Entering June 1996-June 1999 (N = 1,163)

Table 1: Descriptive Statistics and Bivariate Correlation Coefficients for Variables Used in the Analysis: Brooklyn Treatment Court Participants Entering June 1996-June 1999

Variable	Participant Characteristics	Correlation with Completing 90 Days of Treatment	Correlation with Completing Phase One
Coercion			
Legal: Treatment mandate[a]		.143***	.130***
Misdemeanor mandate	33%		
First felony mandate	53%		
Multiple felony	5%		
Predicate felony	9%		
Legal/Emotional: Current family court case	7% (14% females)	.095***	.098***
Demographic/Socioeconomic Characteristics			
Female	38%	−.011	−.019
Age (mean)	33.2 (9.4)	.112***	.138***
Race / ethnicity			
Hispanic / Latino	38%	−.102***	−.112***
Black / African-American	54%	.092**	.108***
Caucasian or other (other = 1%)	7%	.014	.003
Education: high school graduate?	39%	.020	.028
Employed or in school at intake	18%	.030	.036
Ever homeless?	28%	.006	.020
Substance Abuse History			
Primary drug of choice			
Heroin	36%	−.111***	−.126***
Crack	36%	.112***	.111***
Marijuana	14%	.002	−.019
Alcohol	6%	.010	.031
Other (6% non-crack cocaine, 2% other)	8%	−.016	.016
Number of prior treatment episodes[b]		.025	.013
Zero (0)	51%		
One (1)	27%		
Two (2)	10%		
Three (3) or more	12%		
Criminal History			
Prior misdemeanor conviction(s)	35%	−.029	−.041
Prior felony conviction(s)	20%	.070*	.081**
Neighborhood Characteristics			
Neighborhood social isolation score (mean)	121,396 (48,063)	−.044	−.043
Percentage black in neighborhood (mean)	53.7% (32.3%)	.018	.063*
Participation Immediately After Program Entry			
Attended treatment within 30 days	69%	.265***	.238***
Warranted within 30 days	24%	−.330***	−.281***
Days to first placement[c]	30.7 (65.9)	−.065*	−.062*

Note: N = 1093. Participants with indeterminate Phase One completion status are excluded. For the correlations, N = 1021 to 1093 depending on the number of missing cases. Numbers in parentheses are standard deviations. For all correlations, tau-b coefficients are given, since nearly all relationships are between variables with a small number of categories.
  [a] For the correlation analyses, treatment mandate is coded on a 4-category scale from least to most serious mandate.
  [b] For the correlation analyses, prior treatment episodes is coded on a 4-category scale (0, 1, 2, or 3 or more episodes).
  [c] The distribution of days to first placement has an exceptionally long tail. Thus the *median* days to first placement is X days, Y days less than the *mean* of Z days. For the correlations, the natural logarithm is used to create a more normal distribution.
* p < .05 ** p < .01 *** p < .001

least one prior felony conviction were more likely to complete Phase One. However, this last finding may be spurious. By definition, any participant with the predicate felony treatment mandate must have also had at least one prior felony conviction; and as just noted, receiving a more serious (e.g., predicate felony) mandate is strongly correlated with completing Phase One. The multivariate analyses (below) better discriminate the effects, if any, that are specific to treatment mandate and prior felony convictions. The effect of neighborhood social isolation did not reach statistical significance. Participants living in neighborhoods with a higher percentage of black residents were *more* rather than less likely to complete Phase One. Finally, variables measuring participation immediately after program entry were strongly correlated with completion status. Participants attending their first day of treatment within 30 days of program entry were significantly more likely to complete Phase One (tau-b = .238, $p < .001$). On the other hand, those disappearing on a warrant within 30 days were more likely to drop out (tau-b = $-.281$, $p < .001$). Participants were also more likely to drop out if a longer time elapsed before the case manager could locate a suitable first treatment placement, indicating the importance of the availability of appropriate treatment slots.

Multivariate Analyses

All independent variables were entered into a logistic regression equation predicting the probability of Phase One completion. Table 2 presents results for five different regression models. Due to concerns over multi-colinearity, the following variables included in earlier test models were excluded from the final analysis: annual income, drug addiction severity score, a score for level of alcohol dependence, days to first treatment placement, percentage minority in zip code, and initial court supervision level. Appendix A presents a simple correlation matrix for all independent variables. From the sample, 1093 participants had a clear Phase One completion status. Of these 156 (14%) were excluded due to missing data on one or more independent variables. The most serious data quality problem was that 72 (7%) otherwise analyzable participants had missing zip code information. Hence they were missing data for all variables measuring characteristics of the participant's zip code. Note that homeless participants were *not* excluded based on missing zip code data but were assigned the median for all zip code-based measures.

Model 1 included the two variables measuring court-based coercion. Receiving a more serious treatment mandate ($p < .001$) and having a current Family Court case ($p < .01$) both strongly predicted Phase One completion. This confirms hypothesis 1 regarding the impact of legal coercion. The results also suggest that the theorized relationship should be broadened beyond strictly *le-*

Table 2: Coefficients from the Logistic Regression of Completing Phase One on Select Independent Variables: Brooklyn Treatment Court Participants Entering June 1996-June 1999

Variable	Model 1	Model 2	Model 3	Model 4[a]	Model 5
Coercion					
Legal: Treatment mandate	.375*** (.000)	.443*** (.000)	.452*** (.000)	.566*** (.000)	.126 (.402)
Legal/Emotional: Current family court case	.856** (.005)	1.012** (.002)	.999** (.003)	1.046** (.005)	.598 (.273)
Personal Characteristics					
Female sex		−.378* (.022)	−.189 (.280)	−.106 (.572)	
Age		.043*** (.000)	.041*** (.000)	.036*** (.001)	.049** (.004)
Race / ethnicity[b]					
Hispanic / Latino		−.125 (.361)	−.164 (.259)	−.247 (.118)	
Black / African-American		.131 (.371)	.152 (.326)	.242 (.149)	
Education: high school graduate		−.060 (.702)	−.008 (.959)	−.043 (.810)	
Employed or in school at intake		.301 (.140)	.341 (.110)	.342 (.137)	
Ever homeless		−.023 (.890)	.076 (.662)	.009 (.960)	
Primary drug of choice[c]					
Heroin		−.295* (.022)	−.264 (.053)	−.206 (.155)	−.953 (.064)
Crack		.222 (.085)	.209 (.120)	.318* (.029)	−.571 (.267)
Marijuana		.113 (.521)	.008 (.967)	.021 (.914)	−.439 (.087)
Number of prior treatment episodes		.031 (.670)	.056 (.471)	.122 (.147)	
Prior misdemeanor conviction(s)[d]		−.430** (.006)	−.373* (.024)	−.328 (.062)	−.478 (.087)
Prior felony conviction(s)[d]		.149 (.452)	.124 (.556)	−.009 (.967)	
Neighborhood Characteristics					
Social isolation score in zip code		−3.4E−06* (.035)	−3.4E−06* (.046)	−3.1E−06 (.095)	−1.4E−06 (.596)
Percent black in zip code		.001 (.734)	.002 (.528)	−.004 (.273)	
Participation within 30 Days of Program Entry					
Warranted within 30 days			−1.119*** (.000)	−1.372*** (.000)	−.193 (.603)
Attended at least one day of treatment			.767*** (.000)	.857*** (.000)	.190 (.536)
Completion Status for 90 Days of Treatment					6.120*** (.000)
Constant	−1.123** (.002)	−2.080** (.003)	−2.859*** (.000)	−2.340** (.004)	−5.652*** (.000)
Chi-square	28.584***	93.172***	179.115***	198.537***	801.384***
Change in Chi-square	28.584***	64.588***	85.944***		
Nagelkerke R^2	.041	.129	.237	.270	.782

Note: N = 937 in all models. Numbers in parentheses are p values (2-tailed significance test).
[a] The dependent variable in Model 4 is completing 90 days of treatment. In all other models it is completing Phase One.
[b] Based on a deviation coding scheme. The third (unlisted) category is Caucasian in 85% of these cases.
[c] Based on a deviation coding scheme. The fourth (unlisted) category is cocaine (non-crack) or alcohol in over 85% of these cases, or polydrug or none in the remainder.
[d] Based on N.Y.S. Division of Criminal Justice Services (DCJS) rap sheets. For 47 participants, based on self-report.
* $p < .05$ ** $p < .01$ *** $p < .001$

gal coercion (i.e., the threat of incarceration) to incorporate forms of external pressure that may, for instance, have a psychological/emotional component, such as the prospect of losing contact with one's children. To more concretely indicate the magnitude of these effects, Figure 2 shows the percentages of participants completing Phase One with each treatment mandate and each Family Court status. The Phase One completion rates (when excluding indeterminate cases) were 55% for misdemeanor, 61% for first felony, 69% for multiple felony, and a convincing 84% for predicate felony participants. Also, the completion rates rose from 61% to 80% for participants indicating that they face a pending Family Court case.

On the impact of treatment mandate (which persists in Models 1-4), this finding is interpreted to mean that facing relatively more incarceration time predicts a higher probability of treatment engagement. But as an alternative interpretation, could a more serious mandate have other relevant implications that do *not* stem from the length of the incarceration alternative? In particular,

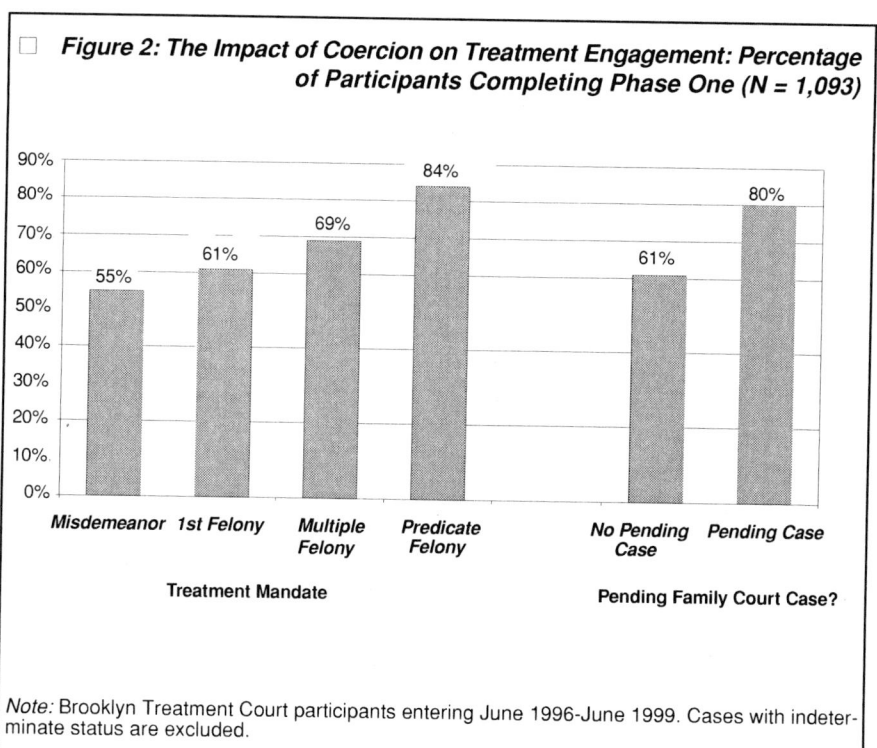

Figure 2: The Impact of Coercion on Treatment Engagement: Percentage of Participants Completing Phase One (N = 1,093)

Note: Brooklyn Treatment Court participants entering June 1996-June 1999. Cases with indeterminate status are excluded.

participants with a more serious mandate tend to receive an initial assignment to a more intensive level of court supervision (e.g., requiring more court appearances, drug tests, and mandatory days in treatment per month). Therefore, it could be that the more intensive supervision level, rather than *legal coercion*, underlies the increased probability of treatment engagement for those with a more serious mandate. In test analyses controlling for initial supervision level, it did *not* affect the probability of Phase One completion, and its addition to the regression model did *not* result in any change in strength in the effect of treatment mandate. This supports our initial interpretation of the treatment mandate finding. (Note that any change in court supervision level *during* program participation would result from compliance or treatment-based considerations and would thus proceed independently of the treatment mandate.)

Model 2 added the variables measuring personal and neighborhood characteristics. Compared with Model 1, there was a statistically significant increase in the chi-square statistic ($p < .001$). As expected, younger participants ($p < .001$) and women ($p < .05$) were more likely to drop out. Race/ethnicity did *not* have a significant effect, even after meeting a .001 significance standard in the bivariate correlations. Further analysis revealed that black participants are significantly older and Latino participants significantly younger than average. Thus the previous bivariate relationship between race/ethnicity and treatment engagement was *not* due to race per se but due to the inter-correlation of race and age.

Of the variables tapping socioeconomic background and social ties, educational background, employment/educational status, and homeless status were all insignificant. Participants whose primary drug was *heroin* were more likely than others to drop out ($p < .05$). Having a primary drug of crack and having prior treatment episodes had no significant effect. Regarding criminal history, participants with at least one prior misdemeanor conviction were more likely to drop out ($p < .01$). This finding is consistent with BTC staff observations that those with a history of nonviolent, low level offending often have a serious personal drug addiction. Finally, as hypothesized, participants living in neighborhoods scoring higher in social isolation were more likely to drop out. The proportion of black residents living in the participant's neighborhood had no effect.

Model 3 added the two variables measuring participation immediately after program entry. Compared with Model 2, there was a statistically significant increase in the chi-square statistic ($p < .001$) and a substantial rise in the Nagelkerke R square from .129 to .237. As expected, disappearing on a warrant within 30 days predicted dropping out ($p < .001$), whereas attending at least one day of treatment within 30 days predicted completion ($p < .001$). In regards to the finding on warrant status, 98% of participants who disappeared on a warrant within 30 days eventually returned (voluntarily or involuntarily).

Hence their lower probability of treatment engagement was *not* due to disappearing forever from program contact but due to disappearing temporarily during a critical period and then never becoming seriously engaged thereafter, even after returning to court custody. It is additionally revealing that although 24% of all BTC participants disappeared on a warrant within 30 days, of those who *first* attended a day of treatment, only 12% *then* disappeared within 30 days.

Along with legal coercion and age, the two post-entry participation variables were the strongest predictors in Model 3. Figure 3 more concretely illustrates the magnitude of these effects. Phase One completion rates (when excluding indeterminate cases) rose from 44% for those not beginning to 69% for those beginning treatment within 30 days of program entry. Also, completion rates rose from 37% for those warranting to 69% for those not warranting within 30 days of entry. And completion rates were 50% for participants aged 16-25, 59% for participants aged 26-35, and 70% for participants older than 35.

After reaching significance in Model 2 ($p = .022$), sex ceased to exert a significant effect in Model 3 ($p = .280$). To explain this, we investigated the inter-correlation of sex with the two variables added in Model 3. Females were more likely than males to go out on a warrant within 30 days (tau-b = $.101, p < .01$) and were less likely to attend a first day of treatment in that time (tau-b = $-.152$, $p < .001$). We also found that females averaged more than twice as many days to first treatment placement as men (17 for females versus 7 for males) which suggests that females may be less likely to begin treatment within 30 days largely due to the greater difficulty that BTC case managers have in placing females. Indeed, when controlling for days to first treatment placement, the correlation between sex and attending treatment within 30 days became statistically insignificant (partial correlation = $.043$, $p = .160$). This means that females and males do *not* have inherently different Phase One completion rates. Females *appear* to have a lower completion rate due to the consequences of taking longer to place. From a policy standpoint, addressing sex-based differences in days to first placement emerges as an important challenge.

Although not to the extent of sex, primary drug of heroin ($p = .053$) and prior misdemeanor conviction(s) ($p = .024$) also weakened in significance after controlling for post-entry participation status.

Due to multi-colinearity concerns stemming from inter-correlations among many of the predictor variables (see Appendix A), we ran a test model (results not shown) deleting all variables that failed to reach statistical significance in Model 3. Variables in the test model were treatment mandate, Family Court status, age, primary drug, prior misdemeanor conviction(s), neighborhood social isolation, warranting within 30 days of program entry and beginning treatment within 30 days of program entry.

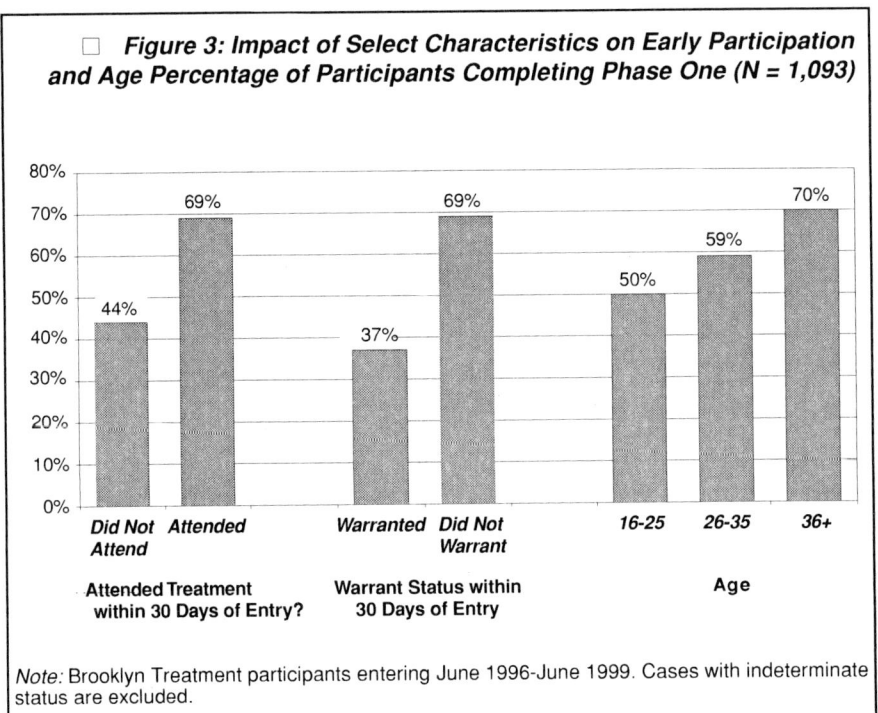

Figure 3: Impact of Select Characteristics on Early Participation and Age Percentage of Participants Completing Phase One (N = 1,093)

Note: Brooklyn Treatment participants entering June 1996-June 1999. Cases with indeterminate status are excluded.

All relationships remained nearly the same as in Model 3, except that primary drug of heroin reached a substantially *more* robust significance level (p = .001).

Model 4 used the same predictor variables as Model 3, except that the dependent variable changed to retention status for 90 days of treatment. Results were generally similar to Model 3. The two post-entry participation status variables appeared noticeably stronger in their effects (from examining Wald statistics not shown), and some of the other variables appeared weaker, falling just under the .05 significance level: primary drug of heroin, prior misdemeanor conviction(s), and social isolation. It is additionally notable that in Model 4, a primary drug of *crack* significantly predicted *retention* rather than dropout (p < .05). This contradicts the common classification of crack as among the most highly addictive drugs.

The purpose of Model 5 was to determine, once a participant has been retained for 90 days of treatment, whether that became the only relevant fact predicting Phase One completion, or did other variables continue to affect progress. In other words, did factors rooted in background participant characteristics or early in-program participation diminish to predictive irrelevance after a certain point, and did retention for 90 days of treatment represent such a point? It was plausible for other variables to become insignificant once it was known that a participant has been retained for 90 days, since it is known that most BTC dropouts fail the program early on. (For BTC dropouts, median time in treatment is 24 days). Nonetheless, from Figure 1, it was determined that approximately 10% *fewer* participants complete Phase One than complete 90 days of treatment, raising the question of whether the outcome for this 10% can be partially explained by any of the above predictor variables.

Statistically, Model 5 mirrors Model 3 except for three changes. The first was the addition, as an independent variable, of retention status for 90 days of treatment. The second was that all predictor variables are *interaction terms*. Treatment mandate is actually mandate multiplied by 90-day retention status, age is age multiplied by 90-day retention status, and so forth. By creating interaction terms, and controlling for 90 days of treatment, the model could estimate the effect of each predictor variable on Phase One completion *once the participant is known to have completed 90 days of treatment*. The third change was that Model 5 was simplified to include only variables that were statistically significant in either Models 3 or 4.

The results show that virtually all predictors from Models 3 and 4 became statistically insignificant in Model 5, including the previously robust predictors of treatment mandate, warranting within 30 days of program entry, and attending treatment within 30 days. The one predictor that exerted a significant effect in Model 5 was age ($p < .01$). Younger participants retained for 90 days of treatment remain disproportionately likely to drop out during the interim period before completing Phase One. Also, although these other findings fall short of a the preferred .05 significance standard, participants with a primary drug of heroin or with prior misdemeanor conviction(s) were disproportionately likely to drop out during the interim period ($p < .10$).

Confirmation/Disconfirmation of the Hypotheses and Implications for Drug Court Policy

First and foremost, the results in this study powerfully demonstrate the impact of what happens *after* the arrest that prompted drug court participation. The three strongest predictors of treatment engagement, legal coercion, warranting within 30 days of formal entry, and attending treatment within 30 days, are all set *after* the initiating BTC arrest. Events occurring within the criminal justice system and within the drug court can greatly affect program outcomes.

Impact of Coercion

As hypothesis 1 proposed, legal coercion was among the strongest predictors. Participants whose treatment mandate implied a longer incarceration alternative were much more likely to complete both 90 days of treatment and Phase One. The ability to divide participants into different *objective* levels of legal coercion, while keeping other program components constant, was one of the key advantages of studying BTC. Most previous research compared voluntary and coerced populations but did not analyze, *within a coerced population*, whether the specific level of coercion made a difference. Our results show that persons seemingly in the throes of a drug addiction are not wholly entrapped by that addiction. Many respond to variations in the rational incentives confronting them.

These results have several potential implications. First, drug courts may benefit from admitting as serious a defendant population as local community values will accept. In this regard, the goals of being "tough on crime" and achieving rehabilitative and fiscal "results" may be in competition. As Figure 2 demonstrated, the Phase One completion rate for the most serious predicate felony subgroup (those with a prior nonviolent felony conviction) was an exceptionally high 84%. Hence, if predicates were excluded from the program, BTC would lose a subgroup that personally benefits at a high rate and provides by far the most efficient return on the financial resources invested. A cost-benefit analysis of correctional savings at the Brooklyn Treatment Court found that average savings per participant were $1,320 for misdemeanor participants, $12,365 for first felony participants, $14,256 for multiple felony participants, and then $57,534 for predicates, over four times the savings for the next highest multiple felony subgroup.[1] Other drug courts are likely to benefit as well from offering the program to their most serious criminal subgroups.

Second, it would be sensible for drug courts to make participants aware of the clear and tangible consequences of treatment failure up front. Young, Dynia, and Belenko (1996) confirm that participant *perceptions* of legal coercion are an important mediating factor. In seeking to generate clear perceptions, drug courts using a "pre-plea" model may be at a disadvantage. In the pre-plea model, instead of requiring a guilty plea and setting an incarceration alternative in advance of participation, the court deliberates on the criminal case only if and when program failure occurs. Although some participants in pre-plea programs may have a sense of the legal consequences awaiting them if they do not complete their treatment mandate, it is likely that many do not. Confirming this expectation, Sung et al. (1999) report that the Brooklyn DTAP one-year retention rate *rose* from 64% to 74% after switching from a pre-plea to a post-plea model. Some policy-makers prefer the pre-plea model, because they consider it better at protecting the legal rights of defendants. In this model, defendants have an opportunity to pursue treatment without having to plead guilty to an offense in advance. Hence defendants who might wish to fight the legal case against them, but are first willing to attempt treatment, do not have to sacrifice the former legal position to obtain the latter rehabilitative opportunity. Without specifically advocating the pre-plea or post-plea models, it is worth observing that the post-plea model, whereby defendants plead guilty and have an incarceration alternative set in advance of treatment, is advantageous for generating a clearer rational incentive to succeed.

Expanding on the questions addressed in this study, a future project would be to explore the impact on court-mandated treatment outcomes of *lower* treatment and graduation requirements. In BTC, incarceration alternatives and graduation requirements, such as minimum time in treatment, are almost perfectly correlated; participants with a longer incarceration alternative are also required to complete proportionately more treatment. For this reason, it is not possible to test whether participants facing the *same* incarceration alternative but *different* graduation requirements average different outcomes. But in theory, it is plausible that graduation requirements enter into the rational calculus of some participants. If drug court graduation is perceived to take less time, participants may become proportionately more likely to remain committed to complete their mandate even after experiencing early setbacks. Of course, drug courts may face institutional limits in what they can change. The courts presumably seek to develop graduation requirements that are an appropriate equivalent to normal prosecution. Also, programmatically, the requirements should be sufficient to make graduation substantively meaningful in terms of what it indicates about recovery. Research indicates that 90 days of treatment is a minimum threshold, but at least one year of treatment is ideal for producing meaningful therapeutic benefits. Nonetheless, for courts failing a high percentage of their participants, it would be useful to know whether adjusting graduation requirements might affect retention.

Besides legal coercion, participants indicating at intake that they had a pending Family Court case were also more likely to become engaged in treatment. We conceive that those trying to retain or regain custody of their children face a form of *legal-emotional coercion*. This coercion is rooted in the threat that failure would pose to the emotional bond between them and their children.

Impact of Early Program Participation

Previous findings on early program participation were mixed, although we hypothesized that it would be an important factor. Confirming hypothesis 4, the results demonstrate that what happens during the 30-day period after program entry critically affects outcomes. Two of the strongest predictors of both retention for 90 days and completing Phase One were whether the participant disappeared on a warrant within the first 30 days post-entry and whether the participant attended a first day of treatment within that same time. Further analysis revealed a more complex relationship. Specifically, we found that once participants attend their first day of treatment, they *then* become substantially *less* likely to go out on a warrant. This critical finding stresses the importance of rapidly placing participants into treatment in order to reduce the probability of their disappearing on a warrant. Also, 98% of participants who do disappear on a warrant within 30 days of entry eventually return, often involuntarily if the police return them to BTC. Hence the problem is not that these participants disappear forever from program contact. Rather, the problem is that warranting early precludes participants from becoming initiated into treatment at a critical juncture. Consequently, after returning to court custody, the more frequent scenario is not subsequent engagement but is subsequent disappearances and returns, followed ultimately by program failure.

Although achieving a rapid placement is clearly paramount, some drug courts may confront barriers beyond their control, such as a lack of appropriate community-based treatment slots. In these cases, other policy initiatives may be possible. These could include requiring more intensive court supervision during the first month of participation: e.g., more case manager contact or more appearances before the drug court Judge. Also, drug courts could have onsite clinical staff administer a brief (e.g., 1- or 2-day) treatment readiness program immediately after participation begins. Depending on program resources, it may be possible to target extra services at those subgroups known to be particularly difficult to place in treatment, such as women in the case of BTC. For example, in the Brooklyn Treatment Court, results reported in this paper led the Clinical Director to develop onsite therapy groups, open to participants who it is believed may have to wait for a significant period before receiving their first placement in a community-based program.

Impact of Personal Characteristics

Age. Confirming hypothesis 2a, this study found that younger participants are at higher risk of dropping out than are older participants. We proposed two explanations, but without supplemental qualitative research, it is difficult to evaluate them. The first was that younger persons tend to have more involvement with deviant peer groups and to be more generally disposed toward deviant behavior. The second was that younger participants have not been abusing drugs for long enough to have grown sufficiently tired of the addicted lifestyle.

Regarding this second explanation, the BTC assessment interview includes a question on the participant's age at the time of first drug use. From this it is possible to construct a variable for the length of the participant's drug use career, from age at first use to age at intake. It would then be possible to test whether length of drug use career predicts treatment engagement. However, this variable turned out to be so heavily inter-correlated with age at intake ($r = .87$, $p < .001$) that the two variables were statistically indistinguishable. Hence we could not reliably test whether older age or longer length of drug use career is the more independently important factor. As a third explanation for the impact of age, perhaps because the court is intervening at the beginning of their adult criminal careers, younger participants tend to be maintained in less intensive treatment services. It may be that such services are not appropriate for these participants. It may be that younger participants would fare better if encouraged to enter more intensive services (i.e., therapeutic communities or inpatient) or if required to have more contact with the court, particularly early in program participation.

Sex. Based on previous research, hypothesis 2b proposed that females were more likely to drop out. This was the case in BTC, but when controlling for days to first treatment placement, the differences disappeared. Since the literature did not contain a compelling theoretical explanation for *why* female sex should matter, in retrospect, it makes sense that sex became insignificant after controlling for confounding factors. The results do suggest that it is critical to place women in treatment quickly. At BTC, females tended to wait more than twice as long as males to be placed, and this affected subsequent outcomes.

Race/Ethnicity. Previous research assessing the relationship between race and retention were mixed, and this study reported no effect. (Although race/ethnicity was significant in the bivariate analysis, this was strictly a result of the inter-correction between race/ethnicity and age, not an inherent effect of race.) Since most BTC participants are minorities, and most attend programs with a heavy minority clientele, minority participants are not isolated within BTC, and programs are likely to be culturally sensitive to their needs. It may be that the effects of race/ethnicity depend heavily on jurisdiction. Other drug courts, perhaps in communities with different demographics, may find that minorities do face race-specific disadvantages.

Socioeconomic and Social Situation Variables. Hypothesis 2c proposed that participants higher in socioeconomic status are more likely to become engaged in treatment. However, educational background had no effect (and in test regressions, annual income also had no effect). This may be due to a lack of variation in the BTC population, since only 11% of the sample had any college training at all, and only 2% graduated from college.

Hypothesis 2d submitted a more theoretical interpretation for *how* social characteristics may affect treatment outcomes. The theory was that participants with stronger *mainstream social ties* would be more likely to succeed. This theory does not hinge on facts about socioeconomic status per se, but is more concerned with the deeper substance of everyday interactions; to what extent do they bring participants in contact with mainstream, non-deviant institutions, activities, and others? Two variables were considered better measures of this than educational background: whether the participant was currently employed or in school at intake and whether the participant had a history of homelessness. But neither was significant. Besides the factor of low social differentiation in the BTC population, it is also possible that in drug courts, legal coercion, supplemented with intensive court supervision, can overcome certain barriers to treatment success that are otherwise rooted in social disadvantages. Pending the outcome of future research, it is conceivable that social disadvantages are generally more influential where treatment is more voluntary.

Substance Abuse History. Hypothesis 2e proposed that participants with a more severe addiction are more likely to drop out. Addiction severity based on self-reported amount, duration, and frequency of use of multiple illegal drugs had no effect in test models. However, primary drug of choice *was* significant. Participants addicted to heroin were more likely to drop out before completing Phase One, although the effect of heroin fell short of statistical significance in the regression of retention for 90 days of treatment. In that analysis, a primary drug of crack was significant in predicting *retention*, not dropout. Although heroin and crack are often grouped together in the most serious addiction category, the results suggest that a *heroin* addiction may be more difficult to overcome. This is actually consistent with other BTC research that when controlling for approximately the same variables as in this study, a primary drug of heroin, but not crack, strongly predicted needing more intensive *inpatient* treatment services (Rempel, 2000). Before generalizing, it may be relevant to consider the importance of methadone policies. BTC has a drug-free approach, and for participants already on methadone at the time of program entry, their dosage must be cut in half before qualifying for Phase One completion. (Methadone users exceeding 80 milligrams at intake are found ineligible for participation.) It is possible that in drug courts with different methadone policies, a heroin addiction would have different implications.

Criminal History. Hypothesis 2f proposed that prior criminal behavior is related to an increased probability of dropout. The results were that prior *misdemeanor* convictions predicted dropout, but prior *felony* convictions had no effect. Discussions with BTC staff suggest that prior *misdemeanor* offending suggests low level criminal behavior designed to support a particularly serious and hard-to-overcome addiction. Staff members explain that persons who are deeply "strung-out" on drugs are not likely to be entrusted to perform major drug sales transactions and therefore not likely to be caught conducting the kinds of drug sales that would give them a more serious *felony* history. This reasoning could not be tested in the current study. A recommendation for future research would be to conduct qualitative studies with participants to disentangle the relationships between criminal history, addiction severity, and treatment outcomes. All research would benefit from continuing to distinguish among *types* of offending (e.g., misdemeanor or felony), instead of using aggregate measures such as total prior arrests or convictions.

Impact of Neighborhood

As hypothesis 3 proposed, higher neighborhood social isolation significantly predicted dropout. As Wilson (1987) theorized, the measures used to tap social isolation most likely serve as proxies for broader neighborhood-based social disadvantages such as poor schools, economic under-development, a lack of stable, regularly employed adult role models, and high rates of crime, substance abuse and other social dislocations. Participants living in socially isolated neighborhoods are likely to be surrounded by fewer interpersonal and institutional supports for their recovery. Relating this to social control theory (see above), socially isolated neighborhoods exert fewer social controls on their residents to engage in mainstream forms of behavior. Although the *personal characteristics* we used to test mainstream social ties (employment/educational status and homeless status) were not significant, the finding on neighborhood social isolation suggests that social control may still affect recovery. But social control may be better measured by aggregate characteristics of the participant's daily social environment than by individual-level indicators, such as employment status. This is in fact the position advanced by Sampson et al. (1999) in studying "collective efficacy" among children. Since to our knowledge no previous study has investigated the impact of neighborhood on substance abuse recovery, this would be an important area for replication. Future studies might generate even more robust results by using better measures of neighborhood, such as census tract instead of zip code. As reported above, the impact of social isolation reached statistical significance at the .05 level in Model 3, with Phase One completion as the dependent variable, but only reached significance at the .10 level in Model 4, with completion status for 90 days of treatment as the dependent variable. Still, the existence of these significant effects is notable, given that zip code is not an ideal measure for neighborhood.

If neighborhood remains significant in other studies, that might suggest a need for more comprehensive policies designed to improve the range of social conditions where substance-abusing populations live. It is beyond the scope of this paper to recommend broader policy changes. However, neighborhood-based policies discussed by Wilson and others include community-based redevelopment, better access to credit for businesses located in poor neighborhoods, housing projects designed to better integrate communities by race and income, and stronger local institutions such as schools, recreational facilities, or community-based social service institutions.

Impact of Retention for 90 Days of Treatment

Over 10% fewer participants complete Phase One than complete 90 days of treatment (see Figure 1). In other words, of those who complete 90 days of treatment, 80-85% go on to complete Phase One. Given this strong relationship, we tested whether, once a participant has completed 90 days, did that become the only relevant fact in predicting whether the participant will go on to complete Phase One. The results confirmed that the previous predictor variables were generally insignificant in their effects on Phase One completion, once knowing that the participant made it to 90 days. The one exception was age: *younger* participants were still disproportionately likely to drop out, even after reaching the 90-day marker. These results indicate that the initial period of participation is when drug courts most need to use information on predictors of engagement to assist those at risk of dropout.

CONCLUSIONS

Level of coercion, rapid initiation into treatment, and older age all strongly predicted treatment engagement in the Brooklyn Treatment Court. Although their effects were less robust, several other characteristics confirmed expectations in predicting dropout, notably heroin as the drug of primary use, prior misdemeanor conviction(s), and higher neighborhood social isolation. Since few previous studies examined predictors of treatment outcomes in court-mandated programs, and even fewer in drug courts, this is clearly a fruitful area for replication. Two of the significant factors in this study, Family Court status and neighborhood social isolation, have received minimal attention in even the larger literature focused on a non-defendant population.

In prioritizing future research, this study points to several specific needs. The literature would benefit from research comparing urban, suburban, and rural drug courts and examining jurisdictions with varying socioeconomic and racial compositions. Although race/ethnicity was *not* significant in Brooklyn, it may be more influential in other communities where treatment services are less culturally diverse. Regarding socioeconomic variables, two factors might explain their lack of significance. First, BTC serves a relatively undifferentiated, low SES population. Second, socioeconomic factors may be generally less influential in a coerced population. External coercion and court supervision may elicit better results among participants who might otherwise be affected by disadvantages related to socioeconomic status.

Among the strongest findings of this study was the relationship between facing *more* incarceration time and treatment engagement. Extending this line of research, it would be useful to establish the full range of incentives to which participants respond. For example, holding the incarceration alternative constant, would participants respond to variations in the extent of their graduation requirements? That is, if a hypothetical treatment mandate of (e.g.) 10 drug-free and sanction-less months was lowered to (e.g.) 7 months, would more participants subsequently be retained through the critical Phase One engagement period, even if the incarceration alternative went unchanged.

In addition to broad incentives, such as the incarceration alternative and required time in treatment, do participants respond to more *specific* program components, such as intermediate rewards and sanctions, treatment modality, and the frequency of required court contacts? For instance, BTC uses an extensive system of graduated sanctions to respond immediately to relapses and other forms of non-compliance. It may be that some sanctions are more effective than are others at motivating participants to succeed after initial non-compliance. Additionally, it may be that certain subgroups are particularly appropriate for more intensive treatment services. It is possible that participants at a higher risk of dropout would benefit from the extra controls provided by an *inpatient* treatment setting. As the significance becomes clearer of the typical prediction variables analyzed in this study, it becomes important for research to look more closely at the treatment and recovery *process* in drug courts. In this regard, there is a compelling need to undertake more qualitative projects that attempt to learn from participants, through focus groups and open-ended interviews, what were the crucial barriers they faced, what factors motivated their success, and how drug courts can improve their services. With the recent proliferation of drug courts nationwide, researchers should have ample opportunities to explore these many questions.

NOTE

1. "The cost-benefit analysis in Rempel (2000) considered (1) incarceration savings from not sentencing participants who graduate, (2) incarceration costs of remanding participants before their first treatment placement, (3) incarceration costs of administering jail sanctions, (4) treatment costs, and (5) difference between the savings generated by the least serious misdemeanor subgroup and the most serious predicate subgroup will remain approximately the same in the final analysis."

REFERENCES

Anderson, E. (1990). *Streetwise: Race, class, and change in an urban community.* Chicago, IL: University of Chicago Press.

Allison, M., & Hubbard, R. (1985). Drug abuse treatment process: A review of the literature. *The International Journal of the Addictions, 20,* 1321-1345.

Anglin, M. D., & McGlothlin, W. H. (1984). Outcome of narcotic addict treatment in California. In F. M. Tims and J. P. Ludford (Eds.), *Drug Abuse Treatment Evaluation: Strategies, Progress, and Prospects* (pp. 106-128). (NIDA Research Monograph 51, DHHS Publication No. ADM 84-1329). Rockville, MD: National Institute on Drug Abuse.

Anglin, M. D., Brecht, L., & Maddahian, E. (1989). Pre-treatment characteristics and treatment performance of legally coerced versus voluntary methadone maintenance admissions. *Criminology, 27,* 537-556.

Babor, T., Dolinsky, Z., Rounsaville, B., and Jaffe, J. (1988). Unitary versus Multidimensional Models of Alcoholism and Treatment Outcome: An empirical study. *Journal of Studies on Alcohol, 49*: 167-177.

Babst, D., Chambers, C., & Warner, A. (1971). Patient characteristics associated with retention in a methadone maintenance program. *British Journal of Addictions, 66,* 195-204.

Ball, J., Lange, W., Myers, C., & Friedman, S. (1988). Reducing the risk of AIDS through methadone maintenance treatment. *Journal of Health and Social Behavior, 29,* 214-226.

Bale, R., Stone, W., Kuldau, J., Engelsing, T., Elashoff, R., & Zarcone, V. (1980). Therapeutic communities versus methadone maintenance. A prospective study of Narcotic Addiction Treatment Design and one year follow-up results. *Archives of General Psychiatry, 37,* 179-193.

Beckman, L. J., & Bardsley, P. (1986). Individual Characteristics, Gender Differences, and Dropout from Alcoholism Treatment. *Alcohol and Alcoholism, 21,* 213-224.

Belenko, S. (1998). Research on Drug Courts: A critical review. *National Drug Court Institute Review 1*(1), 1-42.

Belenko, S. (1999). Research on Drug Courts: A critical review: 1999 Update. *National Drug Court Institute Review 2(2),* 1-58.

Brown, B., Watters, J., Inglehart, A., & Akins, C. (1982/1983). Methadone maintenance dose levels and program retention. *American Journal of Drug and Alcohol Abuse, 9,* 129-139.

CACI Marketing Systems. (1999). *Sourcebook of County Demographics* (12th Ed). Arlington, VA: Author.

Condelli, W., & Hubbard, R. (1994). Relationship between time spent in treatment and participant outcomes from therapeutic communities. *Journal of Substance Abuse Treatment 11*(1), 25-33.

Connor, K., Shea, R., McDermott, M., Grolling, R., Tocco, R., & Baciewicz, G. (1998). The role of multifamily therapy in promoting retention in treatment of alcohol and cocaine dependence. *American Journal of Addictions Winter 7*(1), 61-73.

DeLeon, G. 1984. *Therapeutic community: Study of effectiveness.* National Institute on Drug Abuse Treatment Research Monograph Series; DHHS Publication No. ADM84-1286). Rockville, MD: US Government Printing Office.

DeLeon, G. (1988a). Legal pressure in therapeutic communities. *Journal of Drug Issues*, 625-640.
DeLeon, G. (1988b). Legal pressure in therapeutic communities. In C. G. Leukefeld and F. M. Tims (Eds.), *Compulsory treatment of drug abuse: Research and clinical practice* (NIDA Research Monograph 86, DHHS Publication No. ADM 88-1578, 160-177). Rockville, MD: National Institute on Drug Abuse.
Elliott, D., Huizinga, D., & Menard, S. (1985). *Explaining delinquency and drug use*. Newbury Park, CA: Sage.
Elliott, D., & Menard, S. (1996). Delinquent friends and delinquent behavior: Temporal and developmental patterns. In J. Hawkins (Ed.) *Delinquency and crime: Current theories*. Cambridge: Cambridge University Press.
Farrington, D. (1997). Stepping stones to adult criminal careers. In D. Olweus, J. Block, & M. Radke-Yarrow (Eds.) *Development of Antisocial and Prosocial Behavior* (pp. 359-384). New York: Academy Press.
Federer, M., Boor, P., McKenry, P., & Howard, L. (1986). Factors related to the treatment success of drug addicts enrolled in a residential rehabilitation facility. *Advances in Alcohol and Substance Abuse* 5(4), 85-97.
Feigelman, W. (1987). Day-care treatment for multiple-drug-abusing adolescents: Social factors linked with completing treatment. *Journal of Psychoactive Drugs 19*, 335-343.
Gerstein, D., & Harwood, H. (Eds.). (1990). *Treating drug problems: Vol. 1. A Study of the evolution, effectiveness, and financing of public and private drug treatment systems* (Committee for the Substance Abuse Coverage Study Division of Health Care Services, Institute of Medicine). Washington, DC: National Academy Press.
Gottheil, E., McLellan, T., & Druley, K. (1992). Length of stay, patient severity, and treatment outcome: Sample data from the field of alcoholism. *Journal of Studies on Alcohol* 53(1), 69-75.
Grella, C., Wugalter, S., & Anglin, M.(1997). Predictors of treatment retention in enhanced and standard methadone maintenance treatment for HIV risk reduction. *Journal of Drug Issues, 27*, 203-224.
Harrell, A. & Roman, J. (1999). *Process evaluation of the Brooklyn Treatment Court and network of services*. Washington, DC: The Urban Institute.
Hiller, M., Knight, L., Broome, K., & Simpson, D. (1998). Legal pressure and treatment retention in a national sample of long-term residential programs. *Criminal Justice and Behavior 25*, 463-481.
Hirschi, T. (1969). *Causes of Delinquency*. Berkeley, CA: University of California Press.
Hirschi, T., &. Gottfredson, M. (1983). Age and the explanation of crime. *American Journal of Sociology 89*, 552-584.
Hser, Y., Anglin, M., & Liu, Y. (1990-91). A survival analysis of gender and ethnic differences in responsiveness to methadone maintenance treatment. *The International Journal of the Addictions* 25(11A), 1295-1315.
Hubbard, R., Marsden, M., Rachel, J., Harwood, H., Cavanaugh E., & Ginzburg, H. (1989). *Drug abuse treatment: A national study of effectiveness*. Chapel Hill, NC: University of North Carolina Press.

Inciardi, J. A., & C. D. Chambers, C. (1972). Unreported criminal involvement of narcotic addicts. *Journal of Drug Issues 2*, 57-64.

Jargowsky, P., & Bane, M. (1991). Ghetto poverty in the United States, 1970-1980. In C. Jencks & P. Peterson (Eds.), *The urban underclass* (pp. 235-273). Washington, DC: Brookings Institute.

Jensen, G. F. (1972). Parents, peers, and delinquent action: A test of the differential association perspective. *American Journal of Sociology 78*, 562-575.

Joe, G., & Simpson, D. (1976). Treatment retention for drug users: 1972-1973 DARP admissions. In S. B. Sells and D. D. Simpson (Eds.), *The Effectiveness of Treatments for Drug Abuse* (Vol. 5, Part II, pp. 167-228). Cambridge, MA: Ballinger.

Joe, G. W. (1994). Reducing waiting time for substance abuse treatment does not reduce attrition. *Journal of Substance Abuse 6*, 325-332.

Kornhauser, R. (1978). *Social sources of delinquency*. Chicago, IL: University of Chicago Press.

Laub, J., Nagin, D., & Sampson, R. (1998). Trajectories of change in criminal offending: Good marriages and the desistance process. *American Sociological Review 63*, 225-238.

Lawental, E., McLellan, A., Grissom, G., Brill, P., & O'Brient, C. (1996). Coerced treatment for substance abuse problems detected through workplace urine surveillance. Is it effective? *Journal of Substance Abuse 8*, 115-128.

Leigh, G., Ogborne, A., & Cleland, P. (1984). Factors associated with patient dropout from an outpatient alcoholism treatment service. *Journal of Studies on Alcohol 45*, 359-362.

MacKenzie, D. & Souryal, C. (1994). *Multi-site evaluation of shock incarceration*. Washington, DC: National Institute of Justice.

Maddux, J. F. (1983). Improving retention on methadone maintenance. In J. Inciardi, F. Tims, and B. Fletcher (Eds.) *Innovative approaches in the treatment of XQ abuse: Program models and strategies* (pp. 21-33). Westport, CT: Greenwood Press.

Maglione, M., Chao, B., & Anglin, D. (2000). Residential treatment of methamphetamine users–Correlates of drop-out from the California Alcohol and Drug Data System (Cadds), 1994-1997. *Addiction Research 8*(1), 65-79.

Matsueda, R., & Heimer, K. (1987). Race, family structure, and delinquency: A test of differential association and social control theories. *American Sociological Review 52*, 826-840.

McGlothlin, W., Anglin, M., & Wilson, P. (1977). A follow-up of admission to the California Civil Addict Program. *American Journal of Drug and Alcohol Abuse, 4*, 179-199.

McLellan, A., Luborksy, L., Woody, G., O'Brien, C., & Kron, R. (1981). Are the "addiction-related" problems of substance abusers really related? *Journal of Nervous and Mental Disease 169*, 232-239.

McLellan, A., Luborsky, L., O'Brien, C., Woody, G., & Druley, K. (1983a). Predicting response to alcohol and drug abuse treatments: Role of psychiatric severity. *Archive of General Psychiatry, 40*, 620-625.

McLellan, A., Luborsky, L., O'Brien, C., & Druley, K. (1983b). Increased effectiveness of substance abuse treatment: A prospective study of patient-treatment 'matching.' *Journal of Nervous and Mental Disease, 171*, 597-605.

McLellan, A., Kushner, H., Metzger, D., Peters, R., Smith, I., Grissom, G., Pettinati, H., & Argeriou, M. (1992). The fifth edition of the Addiction Severity Index. *Journal of Substance Abuse Treatment 9*, 199-213.

McFarlain, R., Cohen, G., Yoder, J., & Guidry, L. (1977). Psychological test and demographic variables associated with retention and narcotic addicts in treatment. *International Journal of the Addictions 12*, 399-410.

Moffitt, T. E. (1993). Adolescence-limited and life-course-persistent antisocial behavior: A developmental taxonomy. *Psychological Review, 100*, 674-701.

Mundell, C. (1994). *Drug Abuse in Washington, DC: Insights from Quantitative and Qualitative Research.* College Park, MD: University of Maryland.

Noel, N., McCrady, B., Stout, R., & Fisher-Nelson, H. (1987). Predictors of attrition from an outpatient alcoholism treatment program for couples. *Journal of Studies on Alcohol 3*, 229-235.

O'Donnell, J., Voss, H., Clayton, R., Slatin, G., & Room, R. (1976). *Young Men and Drugs: A Nationwide Survey.* Washington, DC: National Institute of Drug Abuse.

Office of Justice Programs. (2000). *Summary of drug court activity by state and county.* Drug Court Clearinghouse and Technical Assistance Project. Washington, D.C.: American University [On-line]. Available at *www.american.edu/justice/drgchrt1.pdf*; accessed 05/26/00.

Peters, R. & Murrin, M. (1998). *Evaluation of treatment-based drug courts in Florida's First Judicial Circuit.* Tampa, FL: Department of Mental Health Law and Policy, Louis de la Parte Florida Mental Health Institute, University of South Florida.

Petersilia, J., & Turner, S. (1993). *Evaluating intensive supervision probation/parole: Results of a nationwide experiment.* Washington, DC: National Institute of Justice.

Prochaska, J., DiClemente, C., & Norcross, J. (1992). In search of how people change. *American Psychologist 7*, 1102-1114.

Rempel, M. (2000). *Annual research update: The Brooklyn Treatment Court, 1996-1999.* New York: Center for Court Innovation.

Rempel, M. (2000). *Cost-benefit analysis of the Brooklyn Treatment Court.* New York: Center for Court Innovation.

Robins, L. (1980). The natural history of drug abuse. In D. Lettieri, M. Sayers, & H. Pearson (Eds.) *Theories of Drug Abuse.* Washington, DC: National Institute of Drug Abuse.

Rounsaville, B., Dolinsky, Z., Babor, T., & Meyer, R. (1987). Psychopathology as a predictor of treatment outcome in alcoholics. *Archives of General Psychiatry 44*, 505-513.

Sampson, D., Savage, L., Lloyd, M., & Sells, S. (1978). *Evaluation of Drug Abuse Treatments.* Washington, DC: National Institute of Drug Abuse.

Sampson, R., Morenoff, J., & Earls, F. (1999). Beyond social capital: Spatial dynamics of collective efficacy for children. *American Sociological Review 64*, 633-660.

Sansone, J. (1980). Retention patterns in a therapeutic community for the treatment of drug abuse. *International Journal of the Addictions 15*, 711-736.

Sampson, R., & Laub, J. (1990). Crime and deviance over the life course: The salience of adult social bonds. *American Sociological Review 55*, 609-627.

Saxon, A., Wells, E., Fleming, C., Jackson, T., & Calsyn, D. (1996). Pre-treatment characteristics, program philosophy and level of ancillary services as predictors of methadone maintenance treatment outcome. *Addictions 91*, 1197-1209.

Siddall, J., & Conway, G. (1988). Interactional variables associated with retention and success in residential drug treatment. *International Journal of the Addictions 23*, 1241-1254.

Siguel, E., & Spillane, W. (1978). Use of the Life Table Method in determining attrition from treatment. *Journal of the Addictions 13*, 797-805.

Simpson, D. D. (1979). The relation of time spent in drug abuse treatment to post-treatment outcome. *American Journal of Psychiatry, 136*, 1449-1453.

Simpson, D. D. (1981). Treatment for drug abuse: Follow-up outcomes and length of time spent. *Archives of General Psychiatry, 38*, 875-880.

Simpson, D. D., & Friend, J. (1988). Legal status and long-term outcomes for addicts in the DARP Follow-up Project. In C. Leukefield and F. Tims (Eds.), *Compulsory Treatment of Drug Abuse: Research and Clinical Practice* (pp. 81-98.) NIDA Research Series DHHS# ADM88-1578. Washington, DC: Government Printing Office.

Simpson, D. D., Joe, G., & Brown, B. (1997). Treatment retention and follow-up outcomes in the Drug Abuse Treatment Outcome Study (DATOS). *Psychology of Addictive Behaviors, 11*, 294-307.

Speckart, G., & Anglin, M. (1986). Narcotics and crime: A causal modeling approach. *Journal of Quantitative Criminology, 2*, 3-28.

Stark, M. J. (1992). Dropping out of substance abuse treatment: A clinically oriented review. *Clinical Psychology Review, 12*, 93-116.

Steer, R. A. (1980). Psychosocial correlates of retention in methadone maintenance. *International Journal of the Addictions, 15*, 1003-1009.

Steer, R. A. (1983a). Retention of driving-under-the influence offenders in alcoholism treatment. *Drug and Alcohol Dependence, 12*, 93-96.

Steer, R. A. (1983b). Retention in drug-free counseling. *International Journal of the Addictions 18*, 1109-1114.

Sung, H., Tabachnick, C., & Feng, L. (1999). *Drug treatment alternative-to-prison ninth annual* report. Brooklyn, NY: Kings County District Attorney's Office.

Szapocznik, J., & Ladner, R. (1977). Factors related to successful retention in methadone maintenance: A review. *International Journal of the Addictions 12*, 1067-1085.

Taxman, F. S. (1998). *Reducing recidivism through a seamless system of care: Components of effective treatment, supervision, and transition services in the community.* Greenbelt, MD: Washington/Baltimore HIDTA Project.

Taxman, F. S., Kubu, B., & DeStefano, C. (1999). *Treatment as crime control: Impact of substance abuse treatment on the individual offending rates of hard-core substance abusing offenders.* Greenbelt, MD: Washington/Baltimore HIDTA Project.

Thornberry, T., Lizotte, A., Krohn, M., Farnworth, M., & Jang, S. (1994). Delinquent peers, beliefs, and delinquent behavior: A longitudinal test of Interactional Theory. *Criminology, 32*, 47-84.

Trone, J., & Young, D. (1996). *Bridging drug treatment and criminal justice.* New York: Vera Institute of Justice.

Wilson, W. (1987). *The truly disadvantaged.* Chicago, IL: University of Chicago Press.

Wilson, W. (1997). *When work disappears: The world of the new urban poor.* New York: Vintage Books.

Wish, E., & Gropper, B. (1990). Drug testing by the criminal justice system: Methods and applications. In M. Tonry and J. Wilson (Eds.), *Crime and Justice: An Annual Review of Research* (pp. 321-393.) Chicago, IL: University of Chicago Press.

Young, D., Dynia, P., & Belenko, S. (1996, November). How compelling is compulsory treatment? A study of different mandated treatment approaches. Paper presented at the American Society of Criminology Annual Meeting.

Zuckerman, M., Sola, S., Masterson, J., & Angelone, J. (1975). MMPI patterns in drug abusers before and after treatment in therapeutic communities. *Journal of Consulting and Clinical Psychology, 43*, 286-296.

AUTHORS' NOTES

Michael Rempel is deputy research director at the Center for Court Innovation. He is actively involved in research on drug courts and domestic violence courts. He recently co-authored the evaluation of the Brooklyn Felony Domestic Violence Court. Currently, he is on a research team conducting an evaluation of all New York State Drug Courts. He has also published articles on contemporary social theory and the political sociology of advanced industrial societies. In 1997 he co-edited the volume *Citizen Politics in Post-Industrial Societies*, on post-1960s changes in the social structure of advanced industrial societies and their impact on social conflict and public opinion.

Christine Depies DeStefano is a research associate with the Justice Policy Center at the Urban Institute and has been involved in research on substance abuse treatment for offenders since 1996. Currently, she is assisting in the National Evaluation of Juvenile Drug Courts which consists of developing and assessing a conceptual framework for evaluating the success of drug courts when they are implemented in a juvenile justice context. She authored "The Relationship Between Treatment Completion and the Composite Scores of the Addiction Severity Index" and co-authored "Violence in the District of Columbia: Patterns from 1999" and "Treatment as Crime Control: The Impact of Substance Abuse Treatment on the Individual Offending Rates of Hard-core Substance Abusing Offenders."

The authors would like to thank Judge Jo Ann Ferdinand, Adele Harrell, Carlen Rader, Valerie Raine, John Roman, and Michele Sviridoff for their valuable comments and suggestions on earlier versions of the paper. We also thank Judge Ferdinand, Valerie Raine, and other Brooklyn Treatment Court staff for their many insights on the court's policies and participants. This research was supported by a grant from the Center for Substance Abuse Treatment of the Substance Abuse and Mental Health Services Administration to the Center for Court Innovation (CSAT No. 1-UD8-TI11213-01). Prior criminal history data came from the New York State Division of Criminal Justice Services (DCJS). The authors are solely responsible for the methodology used and results obtained from using this criminal history data

Address correspondence to Michael Rempel, Center for Court Innovation, 520 8th Avenue, 18th Floor, New York, NY 10018 (E-mail: mrempel@courts.state.ny.us).

Appendix A: Intercorrelations of Independent Variables Used in the Logistic Regression Analysis: Brooklyn Treatment Court Participants Entering June 1996–June 1999

	(1)	(2)	(3)	(4)	(5)	(6)	(7)	(8)	(9)	(10)	(11)	(12)	(13)	(14)	(15)	(16)	(17)	(18)
(1) Treatment mandate	—																	
(2) Current family court case	−.039	—																
(3) Female sex	.020	.227	—															
(4) Age	−.056	−.001	.099	—														
(5) Hispanic / Latino	−.053	−.024	−.211	−.258	—													
(6) Black / African-American	.091	.046	.202	.233	−.862	—												
(7) High school graduate	−.071	−.007	−.024	.207	−.197	.142	—											
(8) Employed or in school	.001	−.082	−.255	−.166	.074	−.097	.075	—										
(9) Ever homeless	.008	.074	.132	.074	−.063	.080	−.093	−.142	—									
(10) Prim drug of heroin	.077	−.047	.000	.031	.363	−.378	−.037	−.090	.042	—								
(11) Prim drug of crack	−.026	.114	.267	.182	−.314	.352	.059	−.148	.095	−.559	—							
(12) Prim drug of marijuana	−.004	−.042	−.239	−.440	.012	−.008	−.071	.220	−.106	−.298	−.310	—						
(13) Prior treatment episodes	−.035	.129	.129	.161	−.085	.062	.089	−.122	.168	.119	.084	−.239	—					
(14) Prior misdemeanor cv(s)	.003	.008	.139	.185	−.074	.081	.030	−.140	.114	.022	.089	−.138	.068	—				
(15) Prior felony cv(s)	.322	−.043	.104	.087	.078	−.048	.001	−.061	.077	.078	.007	−.109	.087	.207	—			
(16) Social isolation	.014	.004	−.027	−.045	.111	.029	−.144	−.020	.021	.041	.031	.018	.006	−.049	−.062	—		
(17) % black in neighborhood	−.024	.067	.167	.209	−.469	.600	.053	−.069	.089	−.224	.288	−.048	.054	.006	−.041	.255	—	
(18) Warranted w/in 30 days	−.107	.018	.115	.017	−.064	.068	.000	−.058	.072	−.005	.035	−.058	.037	.062	−.065	.028	.050	—
(19) Attended w/in 30 days	−.037	.013	−.161	.012	.013	.004	−.037	.013	−.073	−.084	.011	.104	−.079	−.104	−.081	.004	−.033	−.331

Note: N = 937. Coefficients are simple Pearson's R correlations. Cases are those included in the logistic regression models reported in Table 2.

Index

Abuse history, engagement and, 91-93,99,114
Addiction Severity Index (ASI), 66-67
African-American male clients, enhanced-services program, 45-61
Alternatives to incarceration, 5-10. *See also* Drug courts
American University Drug Court Clearinghouse and Technical Assistance Project, 8

Broward Community College, 63-72

California Proposition 36, 7
Case management, race/gender issues in, 50
Center for Court Innovation, 87-124
Children's perceptions, 22
Criminal history, 67,93,99,114-115
Criminality, risk factors for, 16
Criminal justice system involvement, family, 16
Culturally enhanced programs, 45-61. *See also* Race/gender issues

Doran, Hon. Arthur J., 9
"Dosage" of treatment, 63-72. *See also* Treatment "dosage"
Dowery-Rodriguez, Hon. Brenda, 9
Drug Court Clearinghouse and Technical Assistance Project (American University), 8
Drug courts
  in California, 7
  client demographics, 17
  families and, 8,11-43. *See also* Drug Court Strengthening Families program; Family *entries*
  key components of, 6-8
  origins of, 5
  participant's perspective on, 6-7
Drug Court Strengthening Families program, 11-43
  outcome evaluation, 22-35
    discussion, 33-35
    methods, 22-25
    results, 25-33
  process evaluation, 18-24
    methods, 18-19
    results, 19-24
  program need, 13-18
    high-risk children, 13-16
    local level results, 16-18
Duration of treatment, 63-72

Education/training, 80-83
Eligibility, 6
  for Drug Court Strengthening Families program, 21-22
  as limitation of family program, 22-23
Employment issues, 9,73-85
  discussion, 81-83
  historical background, 74-76
  maintaining job, 79-80
  method, 76-81
  obtaining job, 78-79
  upgrading job, 80-81

© 2001 by The Haworth Press, Inc. All rights reserved.

125

Engagement predictors, 87-124
  Brooklyn Treatment Court operations, 95-96
  conclusions, 116-117
  criminal history, 93,99,114-115
  data and methodology, 97-100
  historical background, 88-89
  legal coercion, 89-90,98,110-111
  neighborhood social isolation, 93-94,99,115-116
  participation immediately after program entry, 94,99-100, 111-112
  personal characteristics, 90-91, 98,112-113
  results, 100-116
  retention, 116
  socioeconomic status, 91,113-114
  substance abuse history, 91-93, 99,114
Enhanced-services race-gender program, 45-61
  African-American male clients, 48-49
  case management functions, 50
  data analysis, 53-54
  design and components, 51-52
  discussion, 56-59
  female clients, 49-50
  research design, 52-53
  retention, 54-56
Evaluation, 7-8

Family, as risk factor, 13-14
Family communication, 15
Family composition, 14
Family conflict, 14-15
Family contact, 30-31
Family criminal justice system involvement, 16
Family discipline patterns, 15
Family drug use, 14
Family stress, 16

Female clients, enhanced-services program, 45-61
Friends' problem behaviors, 27-29

High-risk children, 13-16. *See also* Drug Court Strengthening Families program

Incarceration, alternatives to, 5-10. *See also* Drug courts
Integration with criminal justice, 6

Job issues. *See* Employment issues
Judges' perceptions, 22

(University of) Kentucky, 11-43,73-85
Kentucky Drug Court Strengthening Families program, 11-43. *See also* Family *entries;* Strengthening Families program

Legal coercion, engagement and, 89-90, 98,110-111

Miami-Dade County Circuit Court, 5

Neighborhood social isolation, engagement and, 93-94,99,115-116
Nova Southeastern University, 63-72

Parent/child relationships, 15. *See also* Family *entries*
Parent component, of Drug Court Strengthening Families program, 20

Parenting concerns, 17-18. *See also* Drug Court Strengthening Families program; Family *entries*
Parents' perceptions, 22
Participant obligations, 6-7
Personal characteristics, engagement and, 90-91,98,112-113
Political issues, 7
Pregnancy, as dominant concern in female programs, 49
Problem behaviors
 of children, 29,31
 of peers, 27-29
Proposition 36 (California), 7

Race/gender issues, 8-9,45-61
 enhanced-services program, 48-60
  African-American male clients, 48-49
  case management functions, 50
  data analysis, 53-54
  design and components, 51-52
  discussion, 56-59
  female clients, 49-50
  research design, 52-53
  retention, 54-56
 historical background of Drug Courts, 46-48
Recidivism, 63-72
Retention, 54-56
Risk factors
 for criminality, 16
 for drug use, 13-16
 friends' problem behaviors, 27-29

Sanctions, 6-7
School performance, 31
SFP model, 19. *See also* Drug Court Strengthening Families program
Social isolation, engagement and, 93-94,99,115-116
(University of) South Florida, 63-72
Stress, family, 16
Substance abuse history, engagement and, 91-93,99,114
Substance use
 by children, 29,31
 by peers, 29

Therapeutic jurisprudence concept, 5
Treatment "dosage," 63-72
 discussion, 70-71
 historical background, 64-65
 method, 65-67
 results, 67-69

University of Kentucky, 11-43,73-85
University of South Florida, 63-72
Urban Institute, Justice Policy Group, 87-124

War on drugs, 2-5

Youth component, of Drug Court Strengthening Families program, 20

AN EXCELLENT TEXTBOOK!

Explore the antecedents, onset, and situational and motivating factors behind the violence of today's youth!

KIDS WHO COMMIT ADULT CRIMES
Serious Criminality by Juvenile Offenders

R. Barri Flowers
Criminologist and Crime Writer, Beaverton, Oregon

"An excellent multidisciplinary theoretical base for explaining this most pervasive phenomenon. The text also provides an excellent historical chronology of adolescent offending and the means used to rehabilitate this population. The statistical analysis is most useful in understanding the pervasiveness of the problem."
—Cassandra Bowers PhD, BSW, Coordinator, Wayne State University School of Social Work

This vital book explores the relationship between youth and serious, violent antisocial behavior in America, examining its antecedents, its onset, and its situational and motivating factors. It illuminates the relationship between substance abuse and delinquency and looks at racial and ethnic disparities in youth crime and violence.

Visit the author's website at:
http://barribythebook.homestead.com/Nonfiction.html

$24.95 soft. ISBN: 0-7890-1130-1.
$49.95 hard. ISBN: 0-7890-1129-8.
Available Summer 2002.
Approx. 221 pp. with Index.

Contents
Part I. Exploring Juvenile Crime
- The Magnitude of Juvenile Crime
- Youth and Violence
- Kids, Drugs, and Crime
- School Crime and Violence
- Youth Gangs, Criminality, and Violence
- Dating Violence
- Family Violence

Part II. Explaining Juvenile Crime
- Biological Perspectives on Delinquent Behavior
- Psychological Perspectives on Delinquency
- Sociological Perspectives on Delinquent Behavior
- Intrafamilial Causes and Correlates of Juvenile Delinquency

Part III. Juvenile Crime and the Justice System
- The Police and Juvenile Criminals
- Juvenile Offenders and the Juvenile and Adult Courts
- Juveniles in Custody and Confinement

Part IV. Responding to Juvenile Delinquency and Criminality
- Prevention and Control of Juvenile Crime
- References
- Index

AMEX, DINERS CLUB, DISCOVER, EUROCARD,
JCB, MASTERCARD & VISA WELCOME!
CALL OUR TOLL-FREE NUMBER: 1-800-429-6784
US & Canada only / 8am–5pm ET; Monday–Friday
Outside US/Canada: + 607-722-5857

FAX YOUR ORDER TO US: 1-800-895-0582
Outside US/Canada: + 607-771-0012

E-MAIL YOUR ORDER TO US:
orders@haworthpressinc.com

VISIT OUR WEB SITE AT:

FACULTY: YOU CAN ORDER YOUR NO-RISK 60-DAY EXAM COPY ONLINE

VISIT OUR WEB SITE AT:
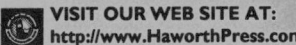

Follow the instructions and receive
your **NO-RISK EXAM COPY.**

A proforma invoice will be sent upon receipt of your request and must be paid in advance of shipping. A full refund will be issued with proof of adoption.

The Haworth Press, Inc.
10 Alice Street, Binghamton, New York 13904-1580 USA

TO ORDER: CALL: 1-800-429-6784 / FAX: 1-800-895-0582 (Outside US/Canada: + 607-771-0012) / **E-MAIL: orders@haworthpressinc.com**

Please complete the information below or tape your business card in this area.

☐ YES, please send me **Kids Who Commit Adult Crimes**
___ in soft at $24.95 ISBN: 0-7890-1130-1.
___ in hard at $49.95 ISBN: 0-7890-1129-8.

- Individual orders outside US, Canada, and Mexico must be prepaid by check or credit card.
- Discounts are not available on 5+ text prices and not available in conjunction with any other discount. • Discount not applicable on books priced under $15.00.
- 5+ text prices are not available for jobbers and wholesalers.
- Postage & handling: in US: $4.00 for first book; $1.50 for each additional book.
Outside US: $5.00 for first book; $2.00 for each additional book.
- NY, MN, and OH residents: please add appropriate sales tax after postage & handling. Canadian residents: please add 7% GST after postage & handling. Canadian residents of Newfoundland, Nova Scotia, and New Brunswick, also add 8% for province tax. • Payment in UNESCO coupons welcome.
- If paying in Canadian dollars, use current exchange rate to convert to US dollars.
- Please allow 3-4 weeks for delivery after publication.
- Prices and discounts subject to change without notice.

Signature _____

☐ **BILL ME LATER**($5 service charge will be added):
(Not available for individuals outside US/Canada/Mexico. Service charge is waived for/jobbers/wholesalers/booksellers.)
☐ Check here if billing address is different from shipping address and attach purchase order and billing address information.

☐ **PAYMENT ENCLOSED $** _____
(Payment must be in US or Canadian dollars by check or money order drawn on a US or Canadian bank.)

☐ **PLEASE BILL MY CREDIT CARD:**
☐ AmEx ☐ Diners Club ☐ Discover ☐ Eurocard ☐ JCB ☐ Master Card ☐ Visa

Account Number _____

Expiration Date _____

Signature _____

FAX

NAME _____

INSTITUTION _____

ADDRESS _____

CITY _____

STATE _____ ZIP _____

COUNTRY _____

COUNTY (NY residents only) _____

E-MAIL _____

May we use your e-mail address for confirmations and other types of information?
( ) Yes ( ) No We appreciate receiving your e-mail address and fax number. Haworth would like to e-mail or fax special discount offers to you, as a preferred customer. We will never share, rent, or exchange your e-mail address or fax number. We regard such actions as an invasion of your privacy.

☐ **YES**, please send me **Kids Who Commit Adult Crimes (ISBN: 0-7890-1130-1)** to consider on a 60-day no risk examination basis. I understand that I will receive an invoice payable within 60 days, or that **if I decide to adopt the book, my invoice will be cancelled.** I understand that I will be billed at the lowest price. (60-day offer available only to teaching faculty in US, Canada, and Mexico / Outside US/Canada, a proforma invoice will be sent upon receipt of your request and must be paid in advance of shipping. A full refund will be issued with proof of adoption)

This information is needed to process your examination copy order.

Signature _____

Course Title(s) _____

Current Text(s) _____

Enrollment _____

Semester _____ Decision Date _____

Office Tel _____ Hours _____

May we open a confidential credit card account for you for possible future purchases? ( ) Yes ( ) No

THE HAWORTH PRESS, INC., 10 Alice Street, Binghamton, NY 13904-1580 USA

(08) (23) (29) 04/02 BIC02